Tales From The Stranger's Room
Volume Two

Compiled and Edited by

David Ruffle

Paperback ISBN 9781780922508
epub ISBN 9781780922485
PDF ISBN 9781780922492

Published in the UK by MX Publishing
335 Princess Park Manor, Royal Drive, London, N11 3GX
www.mxpublishing.com

Cover layout and construction by
www.staunch.com

'There can be no question as to the authorship'

(The following authors mostly all met and posted their work originally on the Holmesian.net forum. Please note that this is not an official Holmesian.net product.)

Mike B *A Socal survivor living in California since 1953. Read the whole Canon in a fortnight and was inspired to write a few poems and other things. He hopes (and succeeds) to put a sense of immediacy in the poetry and give the reader the same thrill of discovery that he experiences when doing the writing. My opinion is that he does.*

Jennifer Emerson *Jennifer Emerson has had a life-long interest in English and American literature (particularly of the 19th century), and grew up watching both the Rathbone/Bruce & the Granada incarnations of Holmes and his Boswell. Some of her favourite authors are Charles Dickens, George Gordon Lord Byron, Sir Arthur Conan Doyle, Washington Irving and Edgar Allan Poe. One of her two current efforts includes research into the Holmes Canon for a collection of short stories centred around Dr. Watson.*

Cassie Parkes *The Diogenes Dilemma and Other Sherlock Holmes Poetry is Cassie Parkes' first terrifying step into the vast world of publishing. A passionate Holmesian, she likes to express her undying love for Sherlock Holmes through poetry every half term, when her sixth form college loosens her shackles.*

Ashley Polasek *Ashley is an honorary English Canadian-born American member of the Sherlock Holmes Society of London. Her love of film and literature has led her into that great cesspool into which all the loungers and idlers of the Empire are irresistibly drained: academia. She is earning her PhD at De Montfort University in Leicester, UK, researching the endurance of Sherlock Holmes in film and television and will be a Doctor of Sherlockiana by 2013. All previous Holmes-related publications are academic and are therefore as dry as a monograph on cigarette and cigar ash. She hopes her efforts at fiction and poetry are a bit livelier. Owns up to liking Barry Manilow. Brave girl.*

Gemma Richardson *Known as the 'evil one' on Holmesian.net, self-styled, mind you. In reality she is a soft-centred gal who spends her time locked away in Avon where she does something or another.*

Carolanne Roe *Carolanne is a Sherlock Holmes obsessive living, eating, drinking and very occasionally working in the West of Scotland. With a passion for Archaeology, computer games and cuddly toy owls, none of which, you will be glad to know, have any bearing on the Holmesian related fiction she writes.*

David Rowbotham *David is a practical engineer by profession and a hopeless romanticist by nature. He is in a perpetual conflict which is bought sharply into focus by the efficient precision of Sherlock Holmes in a brooding gas lit rain swept Victorian London. He is married to a J. Watson lest you doubt his Holmesian credentials.*

David Ruffle *David lives in the UK on the south coast where he* has perfected the art of cider drinking. *A lifelong Sherlock Holmes fan, he published his first pastiche in 2010, 'Sherlock Holmes and the Lyme Regis Horror', and a further collection of stories and drabbles direct to Kindle in 2011. Sherlock Holmes and the Lyme Regis Legacy followed in early 2012, published by MX Publishing. He is rather hopeful there may be more to come. He is a member of The Sherlock Holmes Society of London. Seems they take anybody these days!*

Jane Smith *Jane is a recent college graduate who has had a lifelong passion for all things Holmesian. She enjoys epically battling with college, writing stories and poetry, drawing very amateur cartoons, consuming vast amounts of fiction, playing and listening to classical/Romantic music, wandering aimlessly and pondering the improbable. She leads a busy, busy life in the USA, but finds the time to write the odd occasional piece to the delight of all on Holmesian.net....something all the members are very grateful for.*

Jane Stuart *Jane Stuart realised a couple of years ago that writing poetry was an excellent way to deal with the ups and downs of a demanding but rewarding job. She is grateful to her sons and husband for keeping her in paper and pens, and building her a shed to hide away in. She has not strayed too far from her Lancashire and Shropshire roots.*

Grace Smoczyk *Grace has been a Holmesian for about 7 years and greatly enjoys scratching together stories whenever time permits.(Too infrequently for members of Holmesian.net). She also enjoys playing the violin. She works as a Massage Therapist and lives in the upper Midwest. Which is somewhere. Whereever it is, she married there recently. Ahhh.*

'Singular Deduction' *Although 'Singular Deduction' gave me permission to use her piece, I have had no contact with her for some time....although...I know she likes big words and frequently* *passes back and forth between a large and small vocabulary. She reads, writes and takes photographs plus attempting to play the piano.*

Vida Starčević *Vida Starcevic was born in Zagreb, Croatia, in 1988. She graduated from the University of Zagreb with a degree in English and Information Science. After temporarily abandoning her dream of becoming a librarian, she went on to get her MA in Victorian Studies from the University of Leicester. The first story she remembers writing was about mermaids and wizards when she was nine, but she's branched out since then. She was a participant of The Great Sherlock Holmes Debate, and is one of those people who used to think Sherlock Holmes was a real person. She currently lives in the UK, but mostly on the Internet.*

Paula Trott *Paula has been casually scribbling for the last five years, inspired by her great love of good books! She is currently training for a career in Musical Theatre, having previously worked as a dancer in France and with a circus in Switzerland. Whilst there, she made a point of visiting the sinister but undeniably beautiful Reichenbach Falls. And failed to plummet.*

Mike Wichern *Mike lives in central Illinois. He has a love of history, science, and of course any fiction that combines the two. He is also an avid fan of mystery novels and had a definite interest in the Great Detective from the first time he read the stories at the tender age of sixteen, however long ago that may have been.*

Contents

The Beacon Society

All author royalties accrued from the sale of this book will go to 'The Beacon Society'.

The Beacon Society is a not-for-profit organization.

The Beacon Society is a scion society of The Baker Street Irregulars, an international organization of Sherlock Holmes enthusiasts founded in 1934 by Christopher Morley. The Irregulars (known as the BSI) meet every January in New York City for a weekend of celebration and study. The Beacon Society serves as a link to other scion societies, providing teachers with local resources to bring the magic of Sherlock Holmes to life in the classroom.

Members of the Beacon Society come from all over the U.S. Most of us also belong to one or more other Sherlock Holmes groups. We enjoy each other's company every January and stay in touch on our Internet forum the rest of the year. We joined the Beacon Society because we share a commitment to introducing young people to the pleasure of reading and enjoying Sherlock Holmes.

For more information about how the society works, please visit their website:www.beaconsociety.com

Foreword: 'I hear of Sherlock everywhere'. Again!

Delights, devilment and drollery.

Welcome to this further collection of jottings, vignettes and tales from erstwhile members (and this time, also non-members) of the web forum 'Holmesian.net'. It has been said that any real Holmes enthusiast worth his salt will endeavour to add to the literature of Sherlock Holmes and it is as true today as it has ever been, thankfully so. The pieces gathered together in this collection mostly have their origins amongst the pages of that esteemed forum. A diverse collection of tales and jottings from a diverse collection of folk, but all single minded when it comes to the study of our favourite sleuth.

There is melancholy here; there are laughs, tears and numerous flights of fancy. Did I mention weirdness? The overall content of the forum is varied in the extreme, covering every aspect of Holmes and Watson's lives and careers and along the way we have set ourselves various challenges such as writing pieces on a Holmesian theme for Christmas and Easter. Many of the pieces in this new collection sprang from such challenges and there were many more that could have been included, but had to be omitted for reasons of space etc. (Volume Three anyone?)

I first cut my Holmesian writing teeth through these challenges and one or two others have certainly been inspired by our friendly community to begin committing Holmes pieces to paper   too.

It might be said that we are indeed guilty of degrading a course of lectures into a series of tales and ruined what might have been an instructive and even a classical series of demonstrations by looking at everything from the point of view of a story, but we make no apologies, we enjoyed every moment of it!

I hope, like Watson, that I have achieved some power of selection in my choices for this volume. And as you read, please remember *'Art in the blood is liable to take the strangest forms'* and some of these forms within these pages may be strange indeed!

But, for now…once more, the game is afoot.

The above was the foreword to the original Kindle collection published in June 2011 and also the 2012 paperback edition, published by MX Publishing. Enjoy!

David Ruffle June 2012.

The Battle of Baker Street~Mike B

Grey eyes
Foggy skies
Horses hooves clattering on cobblestone crossroads

Grey eyes seeing keenly into the Night,
Into the darkened hearts of men. . .
Deducing undoing of villainous doings
almost before they begin.

The trail is hot,
The trail is cold -
but fail, He will not!

The tale is old. . .
Since time out o' mind,
Of Mind over matter

Of Mind over murder
Of minding the clues
Most others refuse,

And still more ignore,
But that's what He's for. . .
To get to the deep hidden heart of the matter

The criminals' fragile illusions to shatter;
To make rascals quake at the sound of His name
As much for the Queen as the thrill of the game;

To always know Victory and never defeat -
That is the Battle of Old Baker Street.

A Case of Creation~Jane Smith

When I glance over the records of the many cases in which my friend, Sherlock Holmes, played a part, there is one case which, although it came on the tail end of a far more prestigious international case, was in itself far more worthy of notice, for the singular and terrifying circumstances which surrounded it. Holmes and I had been in Ireland, wrapping up the former case, a matter of great import to the ruling houses of more than one kingdom, and the nature of which was so delicate that even now I must refrain from relating further details of it. Our work in Ireland was completed, but before we returned to Baker Street, I persuaded Holmes to take a brief respite with me, and visit some of the picturesque villages of the Irish coast. With his constant hunger for action, my friend was at first loathe to the idea of what we both supposed would be a peaceful and uneventful holiday. But I described the Irish coast in such glowing terms (omitting the fact that my memories of such were very vague, as I had been there only when I was a small boy) that he was at last persuaded to stop there for a few days before heading back to London.

We travelled northwards in a post carriage, both of us wrapped up in the delight of seeing the verdant splendour of the Irish countryside. Despite the stormy weather of the previous night, the air was now clear, and everywhere we looked was a land of beauty. Pleasant memories of my boyhood holiday crowded in upon me as I gazed upon the green and fertile landscape.

"How wholesome the country is, my dear Holmes!" I cried, breathing in the clear air with pleasure. "If all of London could desert its sordid streets for such a pleasant climate, I fear you would find yourself without an occupation."

"My dear Watson," said Holmes, stretching languidly upon his seat and half-closing his grey eyes, "Your Romantic attitude, though rather old-fashioned, is none the less refreshing. But I should have thought my past cases, such as the affair of the Copper Beeches, would have taught you by now that the real countryside bears little resemblance to the innocent scenes of the pastoral poets. It is in these wild places on the edges of human civilization, and not in the centre of it, that the most atrocious crimes so often take place. But, look! We seemed to have reached our destination, and doubtless it will be proven which vision of the country-side is correct."

Indeed, as he spoke, I beheld over the crest of the nearest hill the smoke rising from the chimneys of the rustic little sea village. Although I knew Holmes was right, I put his gloomy speech out of my head, and resolved to fully enjoy our holiday. A few hours later, we were installed in the quaint little village inn, and were just sitting down to what promised to be an excellent dinner, when we heard a loud disturbance in the street. Holmes was at the window in an instant, and I quickly joined him to behold a crowd of villagers, half-leading and half-carrying the limp form of a young gentleman. It was difficult to guess his age, for, while he did not seem to be above his twenties, deep, haggard creases traversed his pale face, which told of some great sorrow that had aged him beyond his years. It was not merely the bedraggled appearance of his clothing, nor his general air of weakness and exhaustion that at once excited my sympathy; but his weary eyes had such a look of torture, remorse, and fear that no one who saw him could help feeling sorry for him.

As the crowd passed by our window, I heard the young man asking something in a foreign accent. I could not discern what he had said, but I heard one of the villagers answer him distinctly: "Mr. Kirwin is a magistrate, and you are to give an account of the death of a gentleman who was found murdered here last night."

"Come, Watson!" cried Holmes, an eager light springing into his languid eyes. "This promises to be most interesting!"

With that, he flung on his coat and hat and dashed out of the room. With a not unregretful glance at the tasty meal I was leaving behind, I donned my coat and hat and followed Sherlock Holmes to the crowd outside.

"Good day, gentlemen," he was saying to the villagers as I approached, tipping his hat to them as if they were all fine noblemen, and not rustic fishermen. "I see that my friend and I are not the only visitors here today. We are only here on a holiday; but pray tell, what can a right-handed, near-sighted Genevan chemist, who has been lately in London, spent the past several weeks out of society, and came here in a boat, be doing in the village of -----?"

I usually enjoyed the bewildered expressions of people who were unused to my friend's deductive methods, which always appeared the stuff of wizardry until they were explained. But I felt this time Holmes had gone a little too far, for at his words the unfortunate young man grew even paler than he already was, and fixed his red-rimmed eyes on my companion with a gaze of deepest alarm.

"What do you mean by telling me this?" cried the poor devil. "Who are you, if I may ask?"

"My name is Mr. Sherlock Holmes," said he, "And forgive me if I have startled you with my little observations. They are but a habit of mine and are perfectly obvious to anyone who knows how to look. But I see that I shall wear you out with all this talk. You look ready to faint; may I suggest that you step into our lodgings here where an excellent dinner has just been prepared."

"Begging your pardon, sir," said one of the villagers, tightening his grip on the young man's arm. "But this fellow is suspect in a murder, and we are taking him to Mr. Kirwin, the magistrate. I don't know who you and your friend are, Mr. Holmes, but if I were you I shouldn't go about fraternising with criminals like him. Good-day, sir."

With that, the crowd, dragging their prisoner along with them, departed in the direction of a large house at the other end of the street.

Holmes and I, of course, lost no time in following the men at a safe distance. As we slipped quietly into the house and took seats in the back of the large meeting-room, it appeared that the young visitor was being put through a sort of quick preliminary trial. Holmes leaned forward in his seat, pressing his fingertips together, and listening to the words of the witnesses with the utmost attention.

"I went fishing last night, sir, about ten o'clock," said the man who had spoken to us in the crowd, "with my son and my brother-in-law, Daniel Nugant."

The two relatives nodded in the direction of the magistrate.

"When a strong north wind came up," the man continued, "we put in for port. On account of its being so dark last night, and no moon, sir, we didn't land at the harbour, but at a creek about two miles below. I was leading the way, sir, with my fishing tackle, when I struck my foot against something, and fell on my face. My companions came up with their lantern, and imagine my horror when I found that I had stumbled over the body of a dead man!"

The room exploded with the noise of everyone talking at once. I could not contain a slight gasp of horror at the gruesome picture of stumbling over a corpse on the beach, but Holmes did not bat an eyelash. The magistrate managed to calm everyone down, and signalled the speaker to continue.

"We thought, sir, that some poor devil had been drowned, and cast up on the beach by the waves. But when we examined the body, the clothes were not wet, and the body was still warm. We carried it to Mrs. O'Reilly's house, and tried to bring some life back into the poor soul; but he was gone."

"Can you describe the man, Traille?" asked Mr. Kirwin.

"He was a young man, sir, I'd say about five and twenty years of age, and a handsome fellow."

"Were there any marks of violence on him?"

"None that we could see, sir, save the black mark of fingers on his neck; for he'd clearly been strangled."

"Hallo there! Look to the suspect!" cried Holmes suddenly, springing up and gesturing at the young gentleman in question. Several people sprang to his aid, and not a moment too late, for he had nearly crashed to the floor in a faint. I noticed the magistrate view this sudden weakness with a suspicious eye. Holmes crossed to the front of the room and laid a hand on the young man's shoulder.

"Are you all right, my good fellow?" he inquired in a friendly tone.

"You again!" cried Mr. Traille. "Isn't one murderous foreigner enough without more of them poking their nose into our business?"

"Excuse me, but I really must ask what you are doing here," put in Mr. Kirwin, somewhat more politely.

"As some of you already know, I am Mr. Sherlock Holmes," said my friend, "And I am an expert at, as our friend Mr. Traille has so eloquently put it, poking my nose into other people's business. It would be my pleasure to assist you all in the clearing up of this little problem, if you will allow me. But I do not mean to interrupt your proceedings. Pray continue; it is most interesting."

"Mr. Sherlock Holmes!" cried the magistrate in a voice of rapture. "Not Mr. Holmes, the great detective from London?"

Holmes chuckled in his silent fashion. "Holmes the amateur," he corrected. "I sometimes prove useful to the official police."

"Oh, nothing of the sort!" said Mr. Kirwin earnestly. "You will allow me the liberty of shaking your hand? And I suppose this is your friend Dr. Watson!"

"Indeed it is, sir," said I, joining my companion at the front of the room. I must confess I was flattered that Holmes' and my reputation had carried so far.

"I cannot tell you how much I have enjoyed your stories, Doctor!" the magistrate said, shaking my hand warmly. "In fact, I have here in my pocket the latest copy of the Strand magazine, which tells of your thrilling adventure with the naval treaty."

"I observed it the moment we entered your house," said Holmes.

"My cousin in London is so good as to send me copies of the magazine," the Irishman explained.

"That I also deduced, from the appropriately sized envelope, still bearing the postmark, upon this table here," said my friend. "But I had no way of telling if Mr. John Kirwin were your brother, father, son, or other relative. Thank you for clearing that point up."

The magistrate's eyes shone with admiration. "Why, I feel like I'm in a story myself!" he exclaimed. "I cannot tell you what an honour it is to have you both here, despite the unfortunate matter of this murder. Of course you must help with the case. Sit here, near the front, and we shall continue with the witnesses."

I could not tell from his face if Holmes were flattered or annoyed by the Irishman's enthusiasm, but I for one was glad to find an administrator of the law who was, for once, so willing to accept my friend's help. Even Mr. Traille, the suspicious fisherman, became friendlier when he saw that the magistrate approved of Sherlock Holmes.

"I've got something to add to my brother-in-law's account," said the next witness, Daniel Nugant. "Just before Traille stumbled over the body, I swear I saw a boat but a short distance from the shore. There was only one man in it; and I'm sure it was the same boat that this foreigner here landed in this morning!" He pointed an accusing finger at the young gentleman, who trembled visibly and sunk his head in his hands. There was a buzz of conversation again, which the magistrate silenced when he saw that Holmes wished to speak.

"Have you any positive means of identifying the boat?" asked Holmes. "You had a good glimpse of it, I suppose, last night? Despite the lack of a moon, mentioned so kindly by your brother-in-law?"

The Irishman gave him a stubborn look. "Do you think a fisherman like me isn't able to see by starlight?" he asked gruffly. "Of course I didn't conduct a fine inspection, if that's what you mean, but it looked like the same boat, as best as I could judge. And that's good enough for any man!"

"Naturally," said Holmes. "I meant no insult, of course. Do continue."

A woman who said she lived near the shore confirmed Nugant's account of the boat; and Mrs. O'Reilly, the woman who had been mentioned by Traille, confirmed that the dead man had been brought to her house. "We sent for an apothecary, Mr. Kirwin," she said, "But we were too late. He was dead before he ever crossed my threshold, and I know that for a fact. And such a nice, amiable-looking young lad too! Oh, it breaks my heart to think of him lying there all white and cold!" Covering her face with a handkerchief, the elderly woman dissolved into tears.

"There, there," said Holmes, taking her hand gently in his calming way. "My friend and I will do our best to find the young man's murderer, and see that justice is done. Think of that, my dear lady, and take comfort. Have the rest of you anything to say?"

Several other men gave their opinion of the matter, and it was generally agreed, both from the guilty manner and the sighting of the boat, that the young stranger had been the murderer, and, not knowing the proximity of this town to the coast, deposited his victim on what he supposed to be a deserted beach. In the strong north wind of last night, he had been unable to get far away by sea, and, possibly confused as to his location, and in the morning had returned nearly to the same spot where he had left his victim.

"Yes, doubtless that is what occurred," said Holmes coolly. "All the same I should like to look into the matter a little further. I suppose we may see the body?"

"Of course," said Mr. Kirwin. "It has been brought into the next room and laid out. I'd like to see this foreign fellow's reaction to it, as well."

"Ah yes, this foreign fellow," said Holmes, eying him with a keen gaze. "Tragic, is it not, to commit a crime so heinous and yet be so young. Might I inquire as to your name?"

"My name," said the young man sadly, "Is Mr. Victor

Frankenstein, and I swear to you that I am innocent of this terrible deed. Until today, I have been in the Orkney Islands, doing some research. Oh, why must my life be so full of misery?"

"Stow your whining," said one of the fishermen, leading him roughly by the arm into the room where the body lay. "We don't believe your lies here!"

The sight of the young murdered man struck sympathy in my heart. He looked indeed to be about five and twenty, and though his eyes were closed forever, his young face still had the look of a kind and generous spirit. As the fishermen had said, his neck bore clearly the mark of strong, murderous fingers. When Mr. Frankenstein saw the body, it was evident from his reaction that he knew the man who had been killed. He shuddered convulsively from head to toe, then threw himself at the feet of the dead man, muttering something in a despairing, broken tone. I caught the words "murderous machinations," and "my dearest Henry." Out of respect for his grief, Holmes signaled all the men to withdraw, and closed the door softly behind us.

"Surely young Frankenstein is innocent of this foul deed, Holmes," said I, "for you saw how grieved he was upon sight of the body."

"I have learned, my dear Watson, that it is never wise to base one's analysis entirely on the observation of other people's emotions," said my friend, "Yet there are half a dozen other things which make me certain of his innocence. In fact I suspected it from the moment I saw his pale face. I suppose you will keep this fellow in custody, Mr. Kirwin?"

"I suppose I must," said the Irishman.

"But you have no objection to my speaking to him in private, once he has paid his respects to his late friend in there? Good. Then I must request that you leave Watson and me to work this out on our own. We shall tell you all, once it is finished, but I'm sure you have observed from the stories that I am not used to working for an audience."

The magistrate was obviously disappointed to have to withdraw from the proceedings, but he agreed to Holmes' request. I saw with some amusement that he had brought out a little notebook from somewhere, and had been taking detailed notes on everything that had happened since our introduction. I wondered if my stories of Holmes might soon have a rival recorder.

After a few moments, Holmes knocked softly on the door, and it was opened by Mr. Frankenstein. His wasted frame looked weaker than ever, and his pale face was streaked with tears.

"Henry Clerval was my dearest friend in the whole world," he said hoarsely, wringing his thin hands together. "I had no reason on earth to wish him dead. I suppose that prison and freedom are equally miserable to me, for I am the most unfortunate wretch that ever was born; but, Mr. Holmes, do not lock me up alone with my bitter thoughts! Oh, Henry, Henry, what has become of you?"

"That is exactly what I intend to find out," said my friend. "If you would be so good as to answer a few simple questions, it would help my work exceedingly."

The young man's eyes flashed suddenly, and he drew back from Holmes with a look of sick fear. "I'm sure it's impossible to discover the murderer," he said quickly. "It seems too dangerous, anyway. For God's sake stay out of it, or you'll have us all killed!"

"Now listen to me, my dear Frankenstein," said Holmes sternly. "The only reason anyone else should be killed is if we fail to catch your friend's murderer. You may refuse to help me, but you cannot hinder me, from doing so. What were you doing in the Orkney Islands?"

There was a painful silence in the room as Holmes' cold grey eyes bored into the red-rimmed ones of the young foreigner.

"Research," he said at last, looking away.

"Chemical research, of course," said Holmes. "As I observed in the street from the various splashes of acid upon your forehead and fingers. That was how I was able to say you were a chemist; and it may interest you to know that the location of the acid stains informed me that you were right-handed and near-sighted. There are more stains on your left hand, indicating that you poured acid with your right hand into containers held by your left; and the acid splashed on your forehead indicates that you often had to hold your eyes close to your work. May I recommend spectacles as soon as you return to the city. Your birthplace was evident from your accent; and your stay in London evident from your clothing, which was obviously purchased there recently, though you have not been taking very good care of it. The bedraggled clothing together with your roughly shaven face and crudely trimmed fingernails indicates that you have been living in a relatively rustic and isolated fashion for the past three weeks at least; and, even without the later confirmation of these excellent fishermen, it was clear that you came here in a boat when I observed the marks of thick rope, and a few splinters from a wooden tiller, upon your hands. But I see there is nothing more to be learned here at present. If ennui troubles you during your stay with the magistrate, it might interest you to ask for his copies of the Strand, and look over the few sensational little detective stories contained therein. Good-day."

With that, Holmes shook the young man's hand in farewell, left the room, bid good-bye to the magistrate, and was soon standing with me in the village street, in the soft sunlight of a country afternoon.

"Quickly, Watson!" said my friend, as soon as we were outside. "Those blasted tides will have destroyed most of the evidence, no doubt, but if we hurry down the shore we may learn something yet."

"I must confess that, to me, it looks rather black for young Frankenstein," I said to Holmes as we strode swiftly through the streets of the little village. "Inclined as I am to personally believe in his innocence, he seemed so guilty during the interview that everyone else must suspect him. And then there are the fishermen who saw his boat last night. It is hard to ignore that piece of evidence, surely."

"Ah, but you are wrong, my dear Watson," said Holmes with a glitter in his eye. "The fishermen did not see his boat last night. They thought they saw his boat. There is a difference. A boat seen at a distance on a dark night is a very vague image, which may easily be unconsciously altered to match any number of things one sees during the day. If one considers also the fact that their minds were much excited by the murder, and they were naturally on the look-out for a villain, the boat sighting becomes more subjective still. No, Watson, I think you may leave the boat out of the question."

"What then are the points in his defense that you mentioned?" I queried.

"Oh, they are innumerable," Holmes replied. "Consider this idea of a dead body being deposited on a beach in the middle of a windy night. The villagers think that a foreigner, unfamiliar with the coast, would consider this beach a lonely enough location to be a safe hiding-place for his victim. But it would be a very obliging fellow indeed who would drag his victim's body about the sea with him all night, then go to the trouble of landing the boat in a high wind, so as to deposit the body in plain sight of the entire village. Would it not be far easier to simply push the body into the ocean? There is only one sort of killer who wishes his victim to be found; and that is the man who kills in order to wound the living. Frankenstein's grief at the death of his friend indicates that the killer has accomplished that purpose at least."

"A matter of vengeance," I mused. "What more then, Holmes?"

"Well, you saw the marks of strangulation on the young man's throat. The killer clearly approached his victim from behind, grasped both hands about his throat, and squeezed once. I could see from the shape of the marks that his hands never changed position. Now recall the trembling frame of young Frankenstein, and ask yourself whether his thin scientist's fingers could have so easily choked the life out of Clerval, who, except for being quite dead, appears to be strong and in the best of health."

"But how do you account for his guilty manner?" I asked.

"It is obvious that, while Frankenstein is not the murderer, he is nevertheless very anxious that the world should not learn of the identity of that individual. What his exact reasons for this attitude are I cannot yet say. But, ah! Here we are at the scene of the crime."

We had by this time reached the beach, where a recently landed boat, still wet from the sea, sat upon the sand. Holmes gave a little groan of lamentation when he saw how much evidence had been eradicated by the tide; but he took out his tape measure and began the intricate process of taking those measurements by which he could calculate the height of a man he had never seen. As he worked away, humming tunelessly to himself under his breath, I gazed out into the wild swell of the restless ocean. What fearsome danger had emerged from hence to bring death to this pleasant little village?

"Let us return to our lodgings, Watson," Holmes' voice broke in upon my dark thoughts. "I believe I have learned all that I can from this coast, and we have only to formulate our plan of action."

"What did you observe in the sand?" I asked Holmes as we began our walk back into town. "What sort of man was this killer?"

Sherlock Holmes' face looked very grim as he answered. "Unless my calculations have failed me--which I assure you is an impossibility--the killer is approximately eight feet in height. I fear--but I cannot say what I fear."

He did not need to complete his sentence, for his words had already struck fear deep into my heart. It was clear to me that we were dealing with a criminal who was not of human proportions.

Some of my forebodings dispelled, however, as we

returned to the quaint little village, with the sun sinking into the sea in a beautiful display of color, as if nothing bad had happened to mar the day. Holmes paid a quick visit to the magistrate's house before rejoining me at the inn for a very late dinner.

"So what do you propose to do next, Holmes?" I inquired when we had finished our meal.

"I see nothing we can do at the moment," he replied. "But we had best take a respite now, for when it is completely dark we will have our work cut out for us."

"What do you mean?" I asked.

"Simply this: that our best chance of finding the murderer of Clerval lies with Frankenstein himself. As he is a stranger here, there is nothing in this village by which the murderer could exact further vengeance upon his unfortunate victim. I think it most probable that he is lurking about somewhere, waiting to follow Frankenstein back to Geneva. That journey must take place tonight."

"But Holmes," said I, "Frankenstein is in the custody of Mr. Kirwin, and I do not think he is likely to give him up."

"I know," said Holmes, with a grim and enigmatic smile. "But now, Watson, if you will be so good as to hand me my violin, we will see how much the proprietor of this inn objects to my playing it."

Some hours later, Holmes and I were skulking toward Mr. Kirwin's house in the darkness of the village street. I had been rather surprised by Holmes' plan to break Frankenstein out of custody in order to draw the killer into a trap, but I felt confident that my friend was in the right, and was perfectly willing to take the risk, although he had warned me of the danger. When we reached the house, Holmes whistled three times in perfect imitation of a nightingale. There was a soft creak as an upstairs window was opened very slowly, and a burly-looking man—

evidently the one who had been left in charge of Frankenstein—showed his head at the window. Holmes signaled to him with a gesture, and the next moment, the limp body of the young chemist, tied up with several bed sheets, was being lowered down to us. As soon as we had received him, the man closed the window and joined us silently in the street. We crept a safe distance away, to a homey cottage with a small stable behind. The man led us inside the stable, where a young woman, evidently his wife, was standing near a saddled horse and cart, and holding a lantern.

"I see you did an excellent job of administering the drug I gave you, O'Brien," said Holmes to the Irishman, as he propped Frankenstein up inside the cart. "I am sorry to do it to him, but I could not be sure that he would cooperate with our little plan. He will awake in a few moments, however, so it is necessary that we hurry."

The Irishman grunted in assent, and climbed up next to Frankenstein's limp form, taking the reins in one hand. I heard the clink of coins as Holmes thanked him for his services. A few moments later, we were on the public road, Frankenstein and the Irishman leading the way in the cart, while Holmes and I followed behind at a good distance, pistols at the ready.

"If this murderer is as cunning as I suspect, Watson, he is sure to be aware of Frankenstein's departure, and follow him down this road," said Holmes. "This is a dangerous business, and we must now be all ears and all silence."

The night seemed interminable as we followed the distant creaking of the cart over the Irish hills. Faintly we heard the young chemist awake, and be hushed into silence by his driver. Cart, horse, country, and glimmering stars were all becoming one dark, monotonous blur when I suddenly felt Holmes' iron grip on my arm, and his voice speaking sharply in my ear.

"There, to our right, in that clump of ash trees," he whispered. "For God's sake, Watson, be careful!"

The next moment, there emerged from the trees the most hideous thing I ever beheld. Looming, hulking, bloated beyond the appointed proportions of a man, a horrible monster came charging at us in the fuzzy half-light. His skin was a sickening cadaverous yellow, and his eyes blazed like twin fires of evil. He had apparently seen Holmes and me, for he ran towards us, uttering a yell that will haunt me till my dying day. But an instant later, he was staggering backwards, groaning in pain and clapping a gigantic hand to his reddening forehead.

Sherlock Holmes stood beside me, motionless, his tall, gaunt figure outlined against the greying sky, the smoke rising slowly from the barrel of his gun. And in the split second before I followed up his shot with my own, I caught a glimpse of a Holmes that I had never seen before--a man who, despite all his banter about detective work as the only cure for ennui, inwardly took a deep and noble pleasure in ridding the world of evil. With his one, well-aimed shot, that hideous apparition, that wicked parody of humanity, which ought never to have existed and yet still, did exist, was silenced forever. Holmes was more than an eccentric old fellow with a strange way of amusing himself. He was a hero.

Under the combination of both our shots in his brain, the monster's death throes were quickly over, and he lay in a heap on the road. At the sound of the gunshots, the Irishman and his passenger had come galloping quickly back towards us. Victor Frankenstein stumbled from the seat of the cart, and crumpled in the dirt next to his assailant, sobbing from the shock and exhaustion of a tortured mind.

"Your troubles with this monster are now over,

Frankenstein," Holmes announced. "Now I think my friend and I have a right to know by what dark chains your fate has become connected with his."

The chemist straightened up, wiping the tears from his pale face. "My fate is the darkest that ever befell mortal man," he moaned, still staring at the dead body of the monster. "I was mad, foolish, crazed with the lust of my own ambition. I created this monster, having used my knowledge of science to discover the secret of the origin of life. A thousand times have I cursed that day! Clerval is not the only friend he has taken from me, the vile, thrice-cursed thing! Yet had I not fled from my creation in terror, but instead devoted my efforts to pursuing his downfall, my friends might be alive today. Oh, I am wretched! Wretched!" He flung himself down once more and it was hard to say which sight was more pitiful--the bloody heap of the dead monster or the cowering wreck of the man who had created him.

"Shall I take him back to the magistrate's now, Mr. Holmes?" asked the Irishman.

"No, O'Brien," said Holmes in a quiet tone. "Victor Frankenstein, I am setting you free. You yourself did not murder Clerval, and though your presumptuous acts have been the cause of his death, I do not see that you or he or anyone else will be improved by your spending a moment in jail. Mr. Kirwin trusts my judgment, and I will see to it that O'Brien does not suffer any blame for your escape. You cannot be far from another village, where the inhabitants are unlikely to have heard of this affair, or to recognise you as being connected with it if they have. You can take a post-carriage back to the city, and from there proceed wherever you need to go."

"Bless you, Mr. Holmes," sobbed Frankenstein, kneeling at the feet of my friend. "May your life be happier than mine has been!"

"Be off with you now," said Holmes sternly, lifting the young man to his feet.

The three of us stood in silence as the haggard form of Victor Frankenstein disappeared over the hill-top.

"Holmes," I said, turning to my friend, "Are you sure it is wise to release this man to the world? I agree that he has already been punished sufficiently for his crimes, but might he not create another monster like this one?"

"I think not, Watson," said Holmes. "Victor Frankenstein is a broken man. His heart is not that of a criminal, and I do not think he will ever try any more experiments. It is a pity, really; for had he not aspired to that realm which is God's alone, a mind like his might have done great good for the world. But we have done our duty, Watson, and can be glad in that. Look to the eastern sky, now, and behold that new sun rising golden over the water. I think there is still plenty of time for your country holiday, my dear friend."

Mistletoe~Jane Stuart

Blackmail;

Such a pitiless crime.

The grip on the victim relentlessly tightens;

She pays every time.

~0~

Exposed;

Every secret laid bare.

The victim diminished by every dark detail

He threatens to share

~0~

Mistletoe;

Supreme parasite.

Roots penetrate straight to the heart of the host;

Drink deep and hold tight.

~0~

She studies

The mistletoe bough.

A life, looking over her shoulder at shadows,

Unless she acts now.

~0~

Crime scene:

Spilled cup on the floor.

A body, sprawled lifeless, his features contorted;

Blackmailer no more.

~0~

No words

Really need to be said.

Holmes glances from teacup to mistletoe bough,

Freshly cut, overhead.

~0~

The Adventure of the Gold-Engraved Box~'Singular Deduction'

One of the most memorable cases with which my friend, Mr. Sherlock Holmes, was associated during the time I lived with him in our Baker Street flat was a most singular case; brought to him by our landlady, Mrs. Hudson.

It was a cold a dreary morning. Fog had settled once more over the streets of London. All was quiet and had been for weeks. It was one of those long and rare periods of inactivity which I have found to be most dangerous for my friend, Sherlock Holmes. More than once his eye wandered to the drawer of the desk where his vile drug was kept. I hoped and prayed for some form of activity to draw his overactive mind from the fact that there was nothing to do.

I myself was quite enjoying the tranquility. I took advantage of the peace to work on the narratives of my friend's last case, which I had begun some days before. I was occupied in this when I heard Holmes rise from his armchair and begin to shuffle about the room.

A sense of dread overcame me, and I turned to see Holmes, his forehead pressed against the window, pound his fist against it. I rose, relief flooding through me. He hadn't been about to use *the* drug as I had thought.

"Holmes," I began, but stopped. It would be useless to convince him to calm down. It was better to let him vent his frustration. I resumed my place at the writing desk and retrieved my pen.

Then I heard his pacing once more, and glanced at him out of the corner of my eye.

"This really won't do, Watson." Holmes turned and stalked to the other side of the room. I turned to face him as he continued his rant. "This infernal blanket of fog prevents anything out of the ordinary from occurring. The detectives at Scotland Yard retreat to their homes while criminals roam about, eluding even the slightest bit of observance by the common individual. It's dangerous, Watson, dangerous!"

During this speech Holmes had returned to his armchair and had stretched his feet to the fire. I retrieved the morning paper from the pile on the floor and began scanning the columns in an endeavor to cheer my friend.

"Our friend, Lestrade, seems to have been called in on a case several times this week," I remarked thoughtfully, noting three or four different mentions of his name. Holmes snorted disapprovingly.

"They were but trifles. The theft of a china plate from Bertram's Hotel; the theft and return of Miss Emily Cole's purse; and the death of Mr. Jack Bromsby, who, I have reason to believe, was not murdered but committed suicide," came the reply.

I turned in amazement to look at my friend, who was smoking a cigarette with his back to me.

"But how did you..." I began in wonderment.

"My dear Watson," Holmes began, turning to face me. I saw an amused smile playing across the corner of his mouth as he witnessed my puzzlement. "I simply noticed the paper lying on the floor this morning during breakfast, and took the liberty of reading a few columns." He turned back to the fire and resumed smoking.

I shook my head, grinning. Holmes always enjoyed seeing me puzzle over some obvious detail that I had missed. I chuckled and resumed my reading.

Holmes broke the silence. "I do wonder why Mrs. Hudson is on her way up at this time of the morning."

I realised that my friend's keener senses had heard the landlady coming up the stairs long before my own. "I haven't the slightest idea," I remarked, turning back to my paper.

A few moments later Mrs. Hudson did indeed enter the room. I rose to greet her and noted that she appeared rather confused.

"Why, Mrs. Hudson!" Holmes began, his gaze never straying from the fire. "It is not custom for you to come to our rooms this time of day. What is it?"

I motioned for the landlady to seat herself facing Holmes' armchair. Holmes turned and flashed a small smile at her, then resumed his staring at the fire.

Mrs. Hudson began by saying, "I do hope I'm not bothering you..."

Holmes chuckled. "Bothering me? Ha! As if anyone could bother me when life itself is monotonous!" He resumed his serious expression. "Pray tell what is on your mind. You did not sleep well last night. Something is plaguing you."

The landlady was by now accustomed to Holmes' quick deductions, and this simple one had no effect on her composure. She held up a small, white piece of paper with large writing on it. Holmes leaned forward, took the paper, and examined it thoroughly. It read:

"*Bring the wedding gift you received from Mr. Baylor to Hyde Park to-morrow. The bench near the tallest elm.*"

"Interesting message. No signature. Only a fragment of another piece of paper." He held it up to the light. "No watermark. The message is printed. Does this suggest anything to you, Watson?"

Holmes finished his observations and passed the paper to me.

Looking it over, I replied, "He or she wished to conceal his or her handwriting."

"Brilliant, Watson! Only notice the colour and thickness of the letters. A man wrote this. A strong man with large hands, as he was pressing hard, but not intentionally. It is his natural way of writing."

I smiled at Holmes' praise and returned the note to him.

He tossed it aside.

"I do believe we've deduced all we can from this note, Watson. Go on, Mrs. Hudson."

"I am very confused, Mr. Holmes," Mrs. Hudson stated, clasping her hands on her lap. "I don't even have the gift anymore, and I really have no idea who might want such a thing."

Sherlock Holmes looked rather impatient. "The item in question being...?"

"Oh, yes. I'm sorry," the landlady stammered. "It is a small box, but it's not really a box. I never could figure out how to open it."

"Anything on the outside worth noting?"

Mrs. Hudson thought for a moment. "Not that I can think. There were some gold-colored engravings on it, in the shapes of flowers and leaves. It was very pretty as a decoration, but I pawned it off, along with anything else that was useless to me, over five years ago."

During this narrative my friend's eyes began to shine. I knew he sensed something remarkable about the little mystery presented to us by the landlady, though I couldn't see what. He leaned forward, putting his fingertips together and his elbows on his knees.

"And who is this M. Baylor?"

"Oh, just an old friend of my family, Margaret Baylor. She lived in Derbyshire Street with her large family, but passed on a few years ago."

Holmes nodded and reached for his pipe. He smoked thoughtfully for a few moments. "Was this box of any value?"

Mrs. Hudson closed her eyes. "I do remember wondering if the box was solid gold, but its weight proved otherwise. I took it to the jeweller on Half Moon Street before I sold it, and he told me it was not worth even a shilling."

Holmes leaned back in his chair. I was confused.

"But surely it must be of some value? Although it appears that it is not as valuable as the author of this note makes it seem," I stated.

Mrs. Hudson nodded. "That is why I've come to you, Mr.

Holmes. I would, if I still had the box, have given it away without a thought. But I'm rather curious as to why anyone would want it, seeming as it is not worth anything."

Holmes leaned forward thoughtfully. "But that the author of the note should send a message rather than approach you himself. That is of the utmost importance."

I must admit, I was not following my friend's chain of thought. Glancing at Mrs. Hudson I could see she wasn't either. She was watching the detective, who was again smoking and staring at the fire.

"How did you acquire the note?" He inquired, without a glance upward.

Mrs. Hudson didn't seem to see the significance of the question. The confused look returned to her face. "Why, Billy the page brought it to me last evening."

Holmes turned to me. "Watson, send for Billy immediately."

~*~

Upon my return with the page, I found Holmes, pacing the room in his dressing gown. Mrs. Hudson had gone. Holmes stopped when he noticed the boy, standing in the doorway looking very puzzled.

"Mr. Holmes," the lad said politely.

Holmes nodded. "Billy, the note you gave Mrs. Hudson; how came it to be in your possession?"

He returned to his armchair and motioned for the lad to sit. The boy shook his head and remained standing in the doorway.

"Sir, the message was attached to the front door yesterday evening. I saw it was addressed to your landlady, so I removed it and knocked on the door. I didn't think she had seen it so I jus' gave it straight to her and left." During this speech Billy had removed his messenger's cap and was wringing it nervously in his hands. "Am I in some kind of trouble, Mr. Holmes?"

Holmes was once again staring into the fire. I assumed he

had no intention of answering the boy's question, if he had even heard it. I put my hand on Billy's shoulder.

"Of course not, Billy. You've done nothing wrong."

The lad relaxed and placed his cap back on his head. "Will that be all, Mr. Holmes?"

Holmes grunted from the chair. I thanked Billy softly and he nodded, then returned to his duties. I closed the door when he had gone.

"We seem to be traveling in confounded circles!" Holmes cried, shaking his pipe at the fireplace.

"What else did you learn from Mrs. Hudson?" I inquired, seating myself in the chair opposite my friend.

"Only the name of the pawn shop to which the box was sold," said he. Rising, he went into his bedroom. "I'll be going out, Watson. I suggest you go and examine Hyde Park. Find the bench near the elm that the note refers to."

I rose, confused. I didn't understand why my friend was dispatching me on a seemingly pointless errand. I knew it was useless to question him, though. Holmes always had a reason for everything he said or did.

"Anything else I should be looking for?" I asked, removing my coat and hat from the stand.

"You will know when you see it, Watson," came the reply from behind the closed door.

Shaking my head, I began my long walk to Hyde Park, all the while trying to understand Holmes' reasoning. When nothing came to mind, I gave up and continued on, paying close attention to everything in my path so as not to become lost in the fog.

Holmes has a reason for everything, I concluded. I'll trust that he knows what he is doing. My time at Hyde Park was, I had believed, completely wasted. I arrived and located the elm which the note referred to and its corresponding bench; but, finding the area void of all activity, I seated myself on the bench and began my observations. The fog had begun to lift, yet I noted nothing worthy of reporting to my friend. After a time I became quite bored. I decided to stroll on the path leading to the bench where I was seated, but before I could leave, a large, dark-haired fellow approached me. He seated himself opposite me, and began a casual conversation. I was glad for the distraction, seeming as my afternoon had been almost wasted by idleness, and we chatted as if we were old friends.

We talked for quite some time. He was very friendly, and inquired after my friends, including Sherlock Holmes. I kept the information about his current case to myself; however, thinking it was best for everyone involved.

After a while I determined my time would be better spent at Baker Street, and upon bidding my new friend farewell, I left him seated on the bench. By then the fog had gone and the return trip went speedily.

At Baker Street, I found the sitting room empty. I called for Holmes, but determined he was still out. I went to my writing desk and began a new chapter of the narrative that had been consuming so much of my time.

Mrs. Hudson entered the room with my supper a few hours later. I thanked her heartily and began eating. On her way out, she gave a start as a man pushed past her and entered the room.

"Is Mr. Sherlock Holmes in?" he inquired.

"Not at the moment," I answered. "He is expected back at any time, however," I added, offering to take his coat while he waited.

The man chuckled and twirled his dark moustache between his fingers. "No, thank you, Watson. I will remove it myself, and return it to the trunk in my bedroom."

I began to laugh. "Yet another clever disguise, Holmes."

Holmes smiled. "Mrs. Hudson, please bring my dinner up," he said, as he stepped into his bedroom and closed the door.

A few moments later he emerged in his dressing gown, holding a small, gold-engraved box. The top and bottom appeared to be made of solid gold gold. Each of the four sides had two large and intricately engraved roses, and many long vines and leaves wrapped around the edges. Seating himself in his arm chair, Holmes began a thorough examination of the box.

"Mrs. Hudson's box!" I exclaimed. "However did you find

it?"

"It was not easy. It had been sold three times after the pawn shop." My friend's eyes never left the little box.

"But how did you acquire the information as to where it was?" I asked. "Tradesman do not give out clients information to just anyone."

Holmes chuckled, raising his head to look at me. "I thought of that. I went in disguise, as you know. I hoped to give the impression that I was the original owner of the box and wished to retrieve it. The clerk believed my little act, and after some persuasion, gave me all of the information about it and the woman who bought it."

Mrs. Hudson entered the room with Holmes' dinner. The glint of the gold box caught her eye. She stared at it for a few minutes before leaving, never once emitting a sound.

"I do believe she is rather annoyed with the whole business," I stated, as Holmes moved to the table and began his supper. I seated myself in the chair opposite my friend.

Holmes nodded. "Yes, and I hope to clear up the situation as quickly as possible. Now, what of your time at Hyde Park?"

I began my description of the place at the park where I had spent my morning. I announced that I had noted nothing worthy of his attentions; all the while he acted uninterested. Deciding to keep nothing to myself, I began to describe the friendly man with whom I had talked. This caught his attention, however, and he became alert and stopped eating abruptly.

"His name?"

I was taken aback by the question. I tried to think back to the conversation, but could not recall him ever telling me his name. "I don't believe he told me," I admitted.

Holmes shook his head. "You say he had a dark moustache and hair?"

I nodded, puzzled. What was it about the stranger that had sparked his curiosity?

"And he was large?"

"Very muscular. Tall, as well," I replied.

Holmes' face had turned grave during this conversation. I

became worried as he pushed back his half-eaten dinner.

"This situation grows more and more serious," said he.

I could get no more of him for another hour. He sat in his chair, smoking his pipe and examining the box by turning it over and over. It was very quiet, so I found a book and settled in my own chair.

"Watson."

I looked up from my book. "Yes, Holmes?"

After a slight pause, he replied, "Tell Mrs. Hudson to be sure all door and windows are locked and the blinds drawn."

I was sure she had always done this, but did as he said. Mrs. Hudson was eagerly awaiting developments, but, seeming as my friend had disclosed no information, I had nothing to give.

Returning to our rooms I found Holmes, bent over the box once more. He was running his long fingers over the engravings. I closed the door quietly, so as not to disturb his examination.

"It is the flowers, Watson," he said.

"The flowers?" I went to my friend's chair.

He pointed out the delicate little flower on the left side of the panel he had been examining, then turned it over and did the same on the next panel. They were exactly the same, whereas the flowers on the right were all different. He then began to push gently on each tiny petal.

I watched him work for some time in silence, and had finally resolved to taking up my book when Holmes gave a shout.

"Halloa! I've got it, Watson!"

Like an excited child Holmes pushed in one of the tiny petals on the bottom of the first rose. He turned the box and repeated the gesture, this time on the top of the rose. On the last rose the box made a clicking sound, and Holmes raised the lid.

Inside the lid was another sort of lock, comprised of three different-sized key holes and a combination lock. Holmes gave a frustrated sigh and set the box aside.

"I do believe a visit to the Baylors of Derbyshire Street is in order for to-morrow," he stated, leaning back in his chair and running his hand through his dark hair.

"What of Mrs. Hudson? Do you believe there is any

danger in leaving her behind, if the man at Hyde Park is behind this?" I asked.

Holmes shook his head. "I'll be going alone. You will stay behind and keep Mrs. Hudson in the house." He reached for his pipe again. "However, I do not believe your man is the only one behind this. No, it is much deeper than that." Lighting his pipe, he added, "He is only one small thread of the web..."

At this I heard no more; the phrase was all too familiar."You suspect Moriarty?"

Holmes closed his eyes and drew a deep breath through his pipe. "I suspect no one."

He smoked for some time in silence, his eyes half shut. No matter how hard I pressed him, he would not talk. I bade him good night with no answer, and retired to my room for the night.

~*~

Morning came soon enough, and by the time I emerged from my room Holmes had already gone. I was relieved to find Mrs. Hudson in good spirits when she arrived with breakfast.

"Any news?" She inquired cheerfully.

I shook my head. "Holmes opened the box only to discover another lock," I explained. Not wanting to disclose any more information without his permission, I promptly began to eat.

"Do keep me informed, Doctor," the landlady said before leaving.

I spent the morning tidying my room, and as I worked I tried to contrive a plan to keep the landlady indoors all day. I finally resolved to have Billy run all the errands, and when I dispatched him with his new orders, Mrs. Hudson appeared at the bottom of the stairs. She rushed up to me, looking slightly pale.

"Is Mr. Holmes in yet?" She asked nervously. She held a small paper between her thumb and forefinger.

"No, I'm afraid not," I answered. "What is bothering you?"

She held up the paper. "I've received another note," she said, turning it over to me. It read:

'If orders are not followed in twenty-four hours,
BEWARE.'

I cast a surprised glance at the landlady, who appeared very worried. "I don't believe that silly little box is worth such threats!" She exclaimed, her voice full of anxiety.

"I will give it to Holmes when he returns," I said, placing my hand on her shoulder. She patted it gently.

"Very good, Doctor. I must go back to my duties."

~*~

Sherlock Holmes returned shortly after the incident. He had not been gone very long. I went out to greet him. He appeared to be quite annoyed. Upon my inquiring as to our proposed trip, he closed his eyes.

"Miss Baylor, the daughter, will be arriving at six 'o clock this evening upon my request."

"Was she not at home?"

Holmes shook his head. "I thought of sending a telegram but assumed it would not reach the Baylor household until this morning. By then it would have been too late; I would have already reached the house..." He removed his coat and hat and shuffled to his armchair. "I trust you have not let Mrs. Hudson outside?"

I told him of my plan to have Billy perform all tasks outside of the house, and he smiled. "I knew you would think of something."

I smiled at the praise and remembered the note. Handing it over to him, I watched him read it.

"I assumed it would come to this," he said quietly. "We must keep Mrs. Hudson within our sight at all times."

He said nothing more about the matter, however, and settled in his chair, taking up the little box. He pulled out a few strange-looking tools that I did not recognize and set at once to picking the locks under the lid. Holmes worked at this for little more than a quarter of an hour before he set the box aside, his task completed. All that was left was the combination lock. When I inquired as to how he would set about discovering the combination, he smiled.

"Hopefully Miss Baylor will bring the answer with her when she arrives." He pulled his pipe off the mantle and lit it, and smoked in silence for the rest of the afternoon.

At precisely six o' clock Holmes, who had appeared to be asleep in his chair, startled me by proclaiming he heard the steps of our awaited guest. As I made my way to the door, Mrs. Hudson opened it abruptly.

"A Miss Violet Baylor to see Mr. Holmes," she announced, then retreated calmly.

Miss Baylor stepped into the sitting room shyly as I motioned for her to enter. She was one of the most beautiful women to set foot in our Baker Street sitting room. Her golden hair hung in long ringlets down her back beneath a scarlet-coloured bonnet. A matching shawl draped about her shoulders, and she clutched a small, leather-bound book in her right hand. Her dark eyes glanced around the room nervously, and then finally came to rest on the figure of my friend as he eyed her from his chair.

Holmes rose from the chair to greet our visitor. He motioned for her to sit in the chair opposite his own - facing the window, as was his custom. I watched as he inspected her while she took her seat.

"Have I the pleasure of addressing Mr. Sherlock Holmes, or Doctor Watson?" She inquired, appearing a little distressed by Holmes' piercing gaze.

"I am Sherlock Holmes, and this is my friend and colleague, Dr. Watson," Holmes replied, finishing his evaluation of our guest and leaning back in his chair. After a slight pause, he inquired casually, "Where is your companion?"

Miss Baylor's struggled to hide her surprised expression. "I've heard of your extraordinary powers, Mr. Holmes, yet I am a bit perplexed as to how you've reached that conclusion. Surely you have not seen my companion, who is outside on the street, from your chair!" After regaining her composure, she added, "he is my fiancé, Jonathan Hawkins."

Holmes chuckled. "I do not possess extraordinary powers as you say, Miss Baylor. I simply have trained myself to notice all that I see." He pulled his pipe down from the mantle. "You have splatters of mud all over your right arm; mud splatters are customary of the dog-cart. However, you do not have mud-splatters on your left arm. If you had been alone, you would have sat in the middle of the cart; therefore, I concluded that you had a companion while traveling, which could be the only reason a lady of your social standing would be persuaded to sit to the side of the cart and risk soiling your new dress."

Miss Baylor smiled. "It sounds so simple, now that you have explained it."

Holmes turned to me. "Watson here has remarked the same more than once." He then reached for the little gold box. "Miss Baylor, does this have any significance to you?" He held it in the palms of his hands for her inspection.

The young lady leaned forward. "Not that I can recall, sir," she replied.

Holmes leaned back thoughtfully, eyeing the box. "You may be interested to learn that this box belonged to your grandmother, Margaret Baylor."

"Then how came it to be in your possession, sir?"

Holmes stood. "That is for another time." Opening the box, he added, "I was hoping you would supply me with the combination for this lock."

Miss Baylor emitted a sound I took for a laugh. "I don't see how I could, Mr. Holmes, seeming as I have never before set eyes on that box."

Holmes raised a finger. "Ah! But what of the journal?"

Our lady visitor took a deep breath before beginning. "When I was informed that you had called, and on an important matter of family history, I thought of the journal and how it may be of some use to you."

Holmes nodded. "I see. To whom did it belong?" He

walked to the window and looked out of it, waiting for the rest of the story.

"This journal has been in my family for years - well over three-hundred. As far as I know, Mr. Holmes, it has been passed from mother to daughter for many generations. My ancestors originate from Scotland..."

"It is exactly as I expected!" Holmes cried from his post by the window and waving his pipe. Turning to see Miss Baylor's startled expression; he calmed himself and motioned for her to go on.

She paused for another moment, as if to make sure of the absence of another interruption, and resumed. "The journal has been well kept, though several of the earlier entries signed by a certain...Ailsa Todd, seem to be in some sort of code."

Holmes turned around so suddenly that Miss Baylor leapt from her chair. I noted that our guest's nerves were on edge, and sent Holmes an admonishing look. He barely acknowledged it, however, and returned quickly to the chair. Seating himself, he motioned for Miss Baylor to sit. She did, but she still appeared very tense and ready to spring from the room at any moment.

"Please accept my apologies, Miss Baylor. Watson will tell you that I am prone to sudden movements and exclamations - " his voice trailed off slowly. Suddenly resuming his normal tone, he leaned back. "Now. Is anything known about Ailsa Todd, other than the coded entries?"

Miss Baylor looked at me questioningly. "Yes," she began hesitantly. I nodded, hoping to encourage her, and she continued, a little more at ease. "She was a very trusted maidservant to Mary Stuart, the Queen of Scotland, in 1560."

"Ah ha!" Holmes nearly leapt out of his chair, but upon seeing the strange, nervous look on the face of our guest he restrained himself and rose slowly, abandoning his pipe on the arm of his chair. Miss Baylor clutched the journal so tightly that her knuckles were white. By then it was apparent that the lady possessed some kind of nervous condition, and that she should not be startled more than necessary. I placed my hand gently over hers in an attempt to loosen her grip on the journal. She calmed almost immediately, and then glanced over at Holmes' chair, stifling a laugh. A strange smell was coming from the pipe, and I realized that it was burning a hole in the arm of the chair.

Holmes strode around the room, stroking his chin, lost in thought. I leapt to retrieve the pipe, but it was too late: there was a large black hole in the arm of the chair to match several others that had been put there by other. I shook my head, but the incident was enough to make Miss Baylor laugh aloud. Holmes raised his head in confusion, and I myself stifled a laugh. When he shook his head and resumed his pacing, I returned to my own chair, happy that our guest was feeling a bit better.

"Does that mean anything, Mr. Holmes?" Miss Baylor asked after a few moments, apparently fully recovered.

Holmes leaned against the mantle thoughtfully. "Miss Baylor," he said slowly, turning to our guest, "it means everything."

~*~

Miss Baylor and I sat for some moments in perplexed silence while watching Holmes, who remained standing, turn over all of the newly acquired information in his head.

"Miss Baylor," said I, "I'm afraid Holmes is not going to reveal anything else tonight -"

She nodded understandingly. "I shall leave the journal with you, Doctor, and return to Derbyshire Street then. Please do inform me of how this strange mystery ends," she stated before I showed her to the door. We exchanged some words, and then I left her to her dog-cart and waiting fiancé.

Holmes was still leaning against the mantle when I returned. He had taken up his pipe again, and blue clouds of smoke floated about the room. I had quietly returned to the settee and took up the journal to read a few pages when Holmes turned to me abruptly, as he had been doing since our guest arrived.

"Watson, find the 'S' volume of my index, please." He returned to his armchair and ran his free hand through his hair as I searched for the volume in question.

"Really, Holmes," I ventured to say, "you ought to stop that obnoxious habit of jumping out of chairs and shouting so loudly - I'm afraid Miss Baylor has a nervous condition and was on edge the entire time she was in your presence."

I found the volume and turned around to continue my scolding, but Holmes appeared to have retreated inside himself and was staring vacantly into the fire, the long, thin forefinger of his right hand pulling at the newly acquired burn-hole in the arm of his chair. I sighed and tapped his shoulder, giving up on the scolding all together. He looked at me with a faraway look in his eyes. I waved the book in front of him, a bit annoyed that he had been ignoring me, and he took it quietly and scanned the pages without reply. After a moment he propped the volume open on his knee. I had by then settled in the chair opposite and was reading the first entry of the journal when he called my name.

"Watson," he said, pointing to a paragraph with his pipe stem, "here it is."

I went to his chair and read the entry over his shoulder.

'Stuart, Mary. Queen of Scotland, 1543-1587. Born 1542. Crown jewels discovered missing before flight to England, 1568. Executed 1587, England.'

"The box contains the missing jewels, then?" I ventured.

Holmes laughed. "I do not believe so, Watson. After the queen was executed, many attempts at finding the jewels were made." He clapped the index shut. "Even Scotland Yard, as you may recall, attempted to recover them a few years ago, but without success. The box, however, may contain a clue as to where the jewels were hidden." He set the index aside and rubbed his hands together eagerly. "Now, let us have a look at this piece of history," said he, reaching for the journal.

Holmes occupied himself for over an hour, intently studying the journal. Occasionally he would pause and write something in his notebook. I was naturally curious, yet knew better than to disturb him, so I settled back into my chair to wait. By then I was beginning to feel a bit ill - no doubt due to the large meal I had consumed several hours before. Holmes, as usual when he was on a case, hadn't eaten anything, and I simply could not waste Mrs. Hudson's excellent shepherd's pie.

I must have dozed off, for when I next caught a glimpse of Holmes he was standing near the window, staring out attentively. I rose to join him.

"Any progress?" I inquired, still feeling ill and attempting to suppress a yawn.

Holmes only pointed toward the street. "Your man, leaning against the lamp-post."

I caught sight of the man near the lamp-post across the street. He appeared to be casually observing those around him, but as I looked closer, I noted he was watching our flat. "How long has he been there?"

Holmes turned to me. "I believe since just before Miss Baylor took leave."

I could only guess why the man I had met at Hyde Park would be watching the flat. I became a little nervous for Mrs. Hudson. "Shouldn't we warn Mrs. Hudson?"

Holmes shook his head. "No need to worry her over such a trifle." He drew the blinds and went back to his arm chair. As I returned to the settee, he reached across and passed the worn, red journal to me. "See what you can make of page 2."

I could see nothing unusual about the specified page, which read:

'This day, Queen Mary informed me of her plan to flee Scotland. She is to go to England, in hopes that Queen Elizabeth will show her favour. She wishes for Jinny, Gwen, Blair and I to accompany her. I would be very pleased, but for the fact that dear Gavin and I must call off the wedding until I return. How I shall miss him!'
Ailsa (5)"

I scrutinised the page for a few more moments before commenting, "The only thing out of the ordinary on this page is the number "5" beside the signature. Unless I am mistaken..."

Holmes shook his head. "No, you are correct, Watson. I've

deduced that the "5" simply means page five." He smoked thoughtfully, watching my movements intently.

I turned to page five automatically; on it was a very long string of numbers, each separated by a tiny dash. It read:

"2-3-3-5-8-3-12-6-15-2-20-4-25-1-33-1-35-1-40-3-48-3-56-2-66-1"

"Well, Watson?" Holmes questioned. His notebook once again lay open on his knee. "You know my methods; apply them."

I studied the numbers once more. "It is a cipher, to be sure," I said, attempting to sound confident in my deduction.

"To be sure," Holmes echoed.

I waited for more information from my friend, but he said nothing more. He could be incredibly patient when the mood suited him. I resumed the recitation of my deductions. "Every other number becomes increasingly larger...the first being "2," the third being "3," the fifth being "8" and so on."

Holmes smiled. "Precisely, Watson." He held out his hand for the journal, then leaned back in the arm chair and began to study the page once more, making notes in his notebook.

"The cipher is very simple," he began. "As you know, I am familiar with most types of ciphers and codes; this one is no exception." He finished writing in his notebook and passed it to me. "It is solved by coupling the numbers from the beginning."

I studied the page in Holmes' notebook, filled with several rows of numbers written in his precise handwriting. I began to follow his chain of thought. "The first number corresponds to one word..."

"In this case, a word in the paragraph," Holmes said.

"And the second to a letter in that word," I finished.

Holmes nodded. "See here," he said, moving to join me on the settee and pointing to one of his notes with the stem of his pipe. "The '2' corresponds to the second word, 'day,' whereas the '3' corresponds to the letter 'y'. Therefore, the first letter of the solution is 'y.'"

I nodded and began deciphering the code as Holmes moved back to his chair with his notebook. Coming upon the second letter, though, I ran into a problem. Holmes was puffing silently on his pipe, watching me again. "Holmes, the second letter is "n." Words in English simply do not start with the letters "y" and "n!"" By this time I was quite agitated, not only with the fact that my methods appeared to be failing, but also because, by that time, I was feeling incredibly ill.

"I've come to that, Watson." Holmes took no notice of my flustered mood. Instead, he turned his notebook around to face me. Another collection of letters formed a long string across the page, separated by commas, in this order:

"y, n, r, a, o, e, s, j, b, r, e, a, m"

"Why, it is an anagram," I remarked.

"Correct again, Watson. Now, to solve the anagram." Holmes rose and went to his desk, strewn with papers from past cases and current chemical experiments, and set to work solving the puzzle.

I watched, sullenly, for a few moments before copying the letters in my own notebook and attempting to solve the anagram myself. I wasn't long into it, however, when Holmes startled me by leaping out of the desk chair and hurrying to the table where the abandoned index lay. He strode about the room, scanning the pages quickly. He paused for a moment to place the stem of his pipe on a page, and then returned to the table to retrieve the box.

"What is it, Holmes?" I asked.

A hand-motion served as the reply as he signalled for me to join him. I abandoned my notebook on the settee and went to his side as he stood leaning against the mantle. He lifted the first lid of the box and entered four digits: "1-5-6-6."

"Holmes," I said, becoming annoyed at his ignorance. He had included and even taught me a few things that afternoon, and was acting as if I were not even present. I tapped his shoulder. "What was the anagram?"

"'Year James born,'" He answered, without even a glance in my direction.

"James?" I was thoroughly confused.

"Mary Stuart's only son," Holmes said. He pushed the flower petals as he had done the previous evening.

The next moment seemed as if it were an eternity. I realized that I was holding my breath, my illness forgotten, and I glanced at Holmes, whose eyes were glittering with anticipation. His long, thin fingers prodded the edges of the second lid as he lifted it to reveal a small, yellowed piece of parchment tied with a red ribbon lying on a shallow bed of red velvet.

Holmes went to his arm chair, and I followed absentmindedly, my eyes never leaving the parchment. I was enchanted. To think that a piece of history was lying right before our eyes! I must confess, this cheered me, as I stood behind the chair, looking over my friend's shoulder as he pulled the parchment out of the box and untied the frayed, red ribbon. My hopes were dashed as he unrolled the parchment, only to reveal a series of short scribbles covering the entire page. Holmes, however, was smiling, and he moved the box to the table and went to the desk to retrieve his notebook.

"There must be something more to this than scribbles," I remarked sourly as I took up the box to examine it.

The red velvet lining covered what appeared to be some kind of thick metal - perhaps solid gold. The distance between the outer edges of the box to the inner edge of the lining was nearly four centimeters, making it impenetrable from the outside. The box itself was nearly twenty centimeters from the lid to the bottom; yet the depth of the inside only measured about six centimeters. Why should the inside of the box be so small and shallow, with such a drastic difference in size in comparison to the outside?

Then I knew the answer. There must have been another compartment underneath the red velvet; yet I could see no way to reach it. Pushing the thoughts of my illness aside, I reached inside and pushed on the bottom of the box. It was solid. I reached across to the table where Holmes kept his strange tools and pulled out a small one that appeared to have some resemblance to a knife. I slid the knife along the edge of the velvet lining near the bottom, from corner to corner, to pull the lining away from the bottom of the box.

Holmes must have caught sight of what I was doing, for he rushed at me so quickly that I became startled and dropped the tool. "Watson, what are you doing?"

I explained to him my thoughts, and he dropped to his knees beside the chair and fingered the piece of velvet I had removed from the box before lifting it out himself. I looked inside, and saw a tiny gold door, which Holmes slid aside to reveal a ring attached to the bottom of the box. He took hold of the ring and pulled upward.

The whole bottom of the box came away to reveal another deeper, red velvet-lined compartment. Inside was a black silk pouch, tied with a drawstring.

Holmes took the pouch by the string and lifted it before our eyes. "Watson," he began quietly, "you have found the crown jewels of Scotland."

Suddenly, I felt the most ill I had been since I had awakened, and the last thing I heard as Holmes dissolved into blackness was a metallic clang as the gold-engraved box fell to the floor.

I awoke, feeling as if I had been asleep for some weeks, to the sight of Sherlock Holmes; he hovered over my bed, intently searching my face for some sign of recovery. I felt somewhat better, yet Holmes insisted I stay still while he rang for tea. Holmes had moved me to my bedroom, and situated a chair at my bedside from which he tended to me while I was unconscious (which, as he later confirmed, was precisely twelve minutes).

Holmes returned not five minutes later. "Mrs. Hudson is bringing tea," he announced as he returned to my bedside. "I trust you are feeling well enough for me to leave you?" I noticed then that he had acquired his walking stick in his absence.

"A little light-headed, but I am sure I will be fine," I assured him. "You are leaving?"

Holmes nodded. "Mrs. Hudson is accompanying me to Hyde Park. We may not return for some time."

I nodded my understanding as Mrs. Hudson entered with

my tea. She situated it and bade farewell to me as she and Holmes left. Holmes, as usual, remained silent as he followed the landlady out the door.

As I heard the front door close, a strange feeling poured over me. I leaned into my pillows, hoping and praying for my friends' safety.

~ * ~

After a time, I felt well enough to move to the settee in the sitting room. As I settled in with a copy of the Times I heard the door open and the sound of heavy footsteps on the stair. They were very slow and uneven, as if someone were limping.

Before I had time to think, I turned to see Holmes stumble into the room and lean on his desk near the door, breathing heavily. I rose quickly, wondering what was happening. Before I could offer to help, Holmes had somehow made it to his arm chair and collapsed, without even removing his coat. He didn't utter a sound.

"Holmes! What on earth has happened?" I cried, forgetting about my own recent ailment. Holmes massaged his temples with his fingertips, leaving smudges of dirt and blood on them.

"It's nothing, Watson; please consider your own condition..."

I would not hear of it, and ran to my room for my medical supplies. I could see, both as a doctor and a friend, that Holmes was in serious pain, and it was my job to relieve him of it. I returned and began examination. His overcoat was torn in several places, some revealing cuts and bruises. He also sported a black eye and several bruises on his face and a large cut on the back of his hand bled profusely.

Despite Holmes' pleas to consider my health, I cleansed and bound his wounds. I had done it before, and was sure to do it again in the future. I refused to acknowledge his pleas until he had told me what had transpired during his absence, and what had happened to Mrs. Hudson.

"Mrs. Hudson brought the box to the bench in the park," Holmes said, with a tone of reluctance. "I kept away a safe distance - far enough not to be seen, but close enough to see her and keep her from danger. Then a man appeared, seemingly out of nowhere - your man, Watson."

Here I interrupted him. "Clearly you know the name of 'my man,'" I said angrily. "You seem determined to keep it from me. Who is this man?" I demanded.

I had begun to apply ointment to his eye when Holmes grabbed my wrist tightly. I wondered whether it was to emphasize what he was about to tell me, or to keep me from touching his eye. He closed his eyes.

"Watson," he drew a long breath. "You did not think Miss Baylor's visit strange, when her fiancé stayed outdoors with the hansom?"

"Oh no," I exclaimed, guessing at what he was about to tell me.

Holmes' eyes remained shut. "He knew you would recognise him. Your man," he opened his eyes and released my wrist, "is Miss Baylor's fiancé, Jonathan Hawkins."

My hands fell to my lap unconsciously, as I thought this over. "But why? Is he working for..."

"Moriarty, partially." Holmes finished my sentence. "He wants the jewels more for himself, I believe." He took the ointment from me and began applying it himself. "He has been masquerading as Miss Baylor's lover, now fiancé; because he knew she could give him the key to the box. Not willingly, but unknowingly. She has been nothing more than a pawn in this evil game," he added. "This plan has been carefully orchestrated - from the timing of the notes to Hawkins's 'courtship' with Miss Baylor - it all bears the mark of a greater mind - Moriarty." Holmes finished applying the ointment and returned it to me. "I shall explain later. But now," he rose and removed his torn overcoat, "we are expecting a visitor."

"A visitor," I echoed questioningly. Then I realized that, during the chaos of dressing Holmes' injuries, I had forgotten about Mrs. Hudson. "Wait. Where is Mrs. Hudson?"

Holmes turned to me, his face grave. "Watson," he said slowly. "You have not realised...no, of course not," he mumbled, turning away.

"Holmes," I pressed.

"Mrs. Hudson is being held hostage until Hawkins finds the jewels. He is a greedy man, Watson. He has rushed Moriarty's plan in such a way that it has begun to crumble."

I was shocked. "Whatever do you mean?"

"I didn't arrive to you dead."

At this I was astounded. I had assumed it was a fight with Hawkins, not a murder conspiracy. "He left you for dead?"

Holmes nodded. "However, Hawkins is consumed by greed. And he is a coward. The two work together wonderfully in making the common criminal predictable. Now," he said, rubbing his hands together. "Our visitor has arrived."

He rose slowly and limped to the fireplace, removing the bag of jewels from the mantle and giving it to me. "Put them in your dressing gown pocket," he commanded.

I did as he said as I watched him retreat to his room and close the door, leaving me alone to greet the unknown visitor.

~ * ~

I was seated on the settee when Billy burst in. He barely uttered that a Mr. Hawkins was present to see me when the man himself pushed past him into the room. I thanked Billy and sent him off with a wave of my hand.

"Mr. Hawkins, how nice to see you again," I said, attempting to remain calm and composed. I fingered the bag of jewels in my pocket.

"No need for games, Doctor," Hawkins announced gruffly.

"Games? I'm afraid I don't understand what you mean." I attempted to stall him, hoping Holmes was nearby and that I understood what I was doing. Holmes obviously had a plan, yet I had no idea what it was.

"You must know where the jewels are," he said, inching closer to where I sat. "Sherlock Holmes has been on the case. You knew they were not in the box, yet you sent your landlady to deliver it anyway. Where are they?"

I took a deep breath, in attempt to conceal my anxiety. "I do not know," I said. "Would you care for tea?"

Hawkins reached into his coat-pocket and drew a pistol half way out, just enough for me to see. "I said no games."

I tried again. "I would prefer not to conduct business while Holmes is out," I said. "This is his home, you know."

Hawkins lunged forward and seized my wrist, twisting it hard. Pain shot up my arm and I winced, hoping for Holmes to come to my rescue.

"You must not have heard, John Watson," he said. "Sherlock Holmes is dead. Got into a street fight, he did." He smiled cruelly. "Now, hand them over."

"Dead?" I tried to sound surprised and upset. Apparently he didn't know that Holmes had returned. I coughed. "Alright," I said as calmly as possible, my arm aching with pain. "You may have them. As soon as you inform me where Mrs. Hudson is."

Hawkins growled. "She's safe, that's all you need to know."

Then my assailant unexpectedly loosened his grip on my arm and stumbled backward, a surprised expression on his face. I massaged my arm and turned around to see Holmes in the doorway, his pistol cocked and pointed at the criminal. I breathed a sigh of relief upon seeing my friend, but when I turned around, I stiffened as I watched Hawkins discreetly direct his own pistol at Holmes. He was still shocked by the discovery.

"You should be dead!" He said gruffly. His expression changed from one of surprise to nervousness.

Holmes chuckled. "I was never dead, Hawkins. You knew that. You would never kill a human being so brutally. Beat them up, yes. But not outright murder."

I winced. Holmes was inviting trouble.

"No. To beat a man until he is nearly dead, and then leave him to die, takes some of the guilt away. Am I correct?"

Hawkins returned this with a momentary look of alarm, before becoming angry. He cocked his pistol, and I sent up a silent prayer for Holmes's safety.

"You're a coward Hawkins. A coward. You know that. Joining up with Moriarty gave you an excuse to get what you wanted, because you weren't brave enough to get it yourself."

Hawkins pointed his pistol at me. "I'll shoot your friend if you don't tell me how you got back here in one piece."

I realised then that Hawkins was worried; thinking harder, I realised that I didn't even know how Holmes had come back in his condition. While I was pondering, I felt the cold, clammy metal barrel of the gun on my forehead. I felt sick again, and was afraid of going unconscious in my friend's time of need. I could still see Holmes from my position in the chair. He was smiling.

"You wouldn't shoot Watson. You cannot. As I've said before, you're a coward. I myself would have died were it not for the help of one of my....shall we say, acquaintances?"

Hawkins turned pale, but didn't move or utter a sound.

Holmes turned serious again. "Release Watson," he commanded.

Hawkins shook his head.

Then Holmes, in a split second, raised his pistol above his head and fired. The shot rang through the little flat. I flinched, but Hawkins didn't move a muscle.

All was silent for a moment before Hawkins allowed a smile to creep on his face. "You've wasted a bullet, Mr. Holmes. Shall I make it even?"

Just then, I heard footsteps on the stairs, and a familiar voice called out. "Jonathan Hawkins, you are under arrest for attempted murder and theft!"

~*~

Inspector Lestrade and his men burst into the room to arrest Hawkins. I was feeling very ill, and afraid of slipping into unconsciousness again. I leaned into the chair and closed my eyes. Holmes was by my side in a few short moments, but to me it seemed like an eternity.

"Watson," he said softly as he pressed his good hand against my forehead. "Are you alright? You look quite ill."

"As well as can be expected, I suppose," I murmured.

"I am terribly sorry I had to put you through this, Watson."

I opened my eyes and looked at him, as he moved his hand to pat my shoulder. I could see his apology was genuine. Holmes never was one for apologising.

Before I could say anything, Holmes limped toward Lestrade. After exchanging a few words, the inspector handed Holmes the pistol. Then he returned to me, while Lestrade, his men, and Hawkins retreated.

Holmes seated himself beside me on the settee and arranged the pistol on his lap. "I hope you aren't too badly shaken, dear fellow," he said.

By then I was feeling a little bit better. "I will be fine," I assured him, as I massaged my bruised wrist.

"Good," he said quickly. Then, almost as if he were embarrassed by his concern for me, he turned to the pistol. After inspecting it for a moment, he declared, "As I expected."

Upon my questioning him, he turned the pistol to face me. He had opened the chamber. It was empty.

Relief flooded through me, then anger. "But why carry an empty pistol around? I nearly had a heart attack!"

"As you heard me say, the man is a coward. He only scares people. He has never directly murdered anyone. I never would have hurled those insults at him if I hadn't known it wasn't loaded."

"Yes, but I was still terribly frightened," I pointed out. Then I remembered Mrs. Hudson, and asked Holmes about her.

He smiled. "She should be arriving any moment. Hawkins is not one for keeping secrets under pressure."

~*~

As sure as his word, Mrs. Hudson entered the room

shortly after, escorted by a policeman. She appeared shaken, but unharmed. She seated herself on the chair across from Holmes and me.

"Are you two alright?" she asked, composing herself. "You look as if you've seen a ghost! And Mr. Holmes – what has happened to you? You look terrible!"

I shook my head in wonderment. The kindly landlady had just been returned from a most frightening experience herself, and she was concerned for her tenants' well being! Holmes shook his head, clearly thinking the same thoughts as I.

Mrs. Hudson wasn't finished, and hadn't stopped for an answer. "What is going on? Mr. Holmes, it's clear you are keeping a secret from me."

Holmes smiled and held out his hand to me. I pulled the pouch out of my dressing gown pocket and passed it to him. He opened the bag passed it to Mrs. Hudson, who emitted a sound I took to be a gasp.

"Mr. Holmes! However did you find them?"

"That is a story for another day. But now, I must send for Miss Baylor. Hopefully she will be available to arrive on short notice. Watson, send for Billy immediately."

~*~

Holmes and I spent the evening in peace, musing over the events of the past days. With Hawkins safe under lock and key, we need not worry over Mrs. Hudson anymore. She was free to go about as she pleased; according to Holmes, Moriarty would not dare to emerge from his hiding places until the scandal had quieted, which could be for some time. Holmes had dispatched Billy with a telegram for Miss Baylor. She responded quickly, stating that she would arrive at tea-time the following day.

I pressed Holmes for an explanation of the case and the events that had transpired since my illness that morning, but he would not respond. He lounged in his arm chair, smoking his pipe and starting at the ceiling most of the night, until I re-dressed his wounds and retired to bed. I was surprised to hear Holmes retire shortly after - he rarely went to bed at regular hours. I pondered the events of the day, running them over and over in my head. I could not see how my intelligent friend had come to solve the case in such a short amount of time, or how he could have been sure that Hawkins' gun wasn't loaded. But, I supposed, he would come to that in time. For now, I would have to be content with waiting until tea-time.

~*~

The following morning was uneventful as well. Holmes was not restless, as he usually was the morning after a successfully concluded case; he lounged around as he had the previous evening, following my strict orders to rest. We enjoyed a lovely breakfast of Mrs. Hudson's, grateful that she was feeling well enough to cook, and while Holmes read his copy of the Chronicle I began the first draft of our adventure.

Around two o'clock, Mrs. Hudson ushered Miss Baylor into the room.

"Good afternoon, Mr. Holmes, Doctor," Miss Baylor said. She appeared flustered and tired, though I could see she had noticed my friend's injuries. I invited her to seat herself across from my friend.

Holmes and I nodded to acknowledge greeting. Mrs. Hudson turned to go, but was interrupted by Holmes.

"Mrs. Hudson, do stay and have some tea," he invited.

"I daresay I shall," she replied happily. I ushered her to the place on the settee beside Miss Baylor, but she declined politely and went to pour us our tea.

Holmes cleared his throat. "No doubt you are curious as to why I've sent for you, Miss Baylor?"

Miss Baylor folded her hands in her lap. "Yes, sir, I am very curious..."

I could see something was troubling her, and could guess what it was. I decided not to intrude on her privacy, and questioned her instead. "Is something the matter?"

Miss Baylor looked at me, with a tear in her eye. "My

fiancé had agreed to come to dinner with my family last evening, but he didn't arrive. I haven't heard a word from him since yesterday; it is all very uncharacteristic of him, and I'm worried." She dabbed at her tears with a lace handkerchief. "No need to trouble you with my worries, though."

Holmes shook his head. The news hadn't reached as far as Derbyshire then.

"Miss Baylor," Holmes said gently. "I'm afraid I have some very bad news."

Our lady visitor emitted a gasp and blanched. I was by her side in a moment's notice, ready to help if she fainted. This news would most likely be too much for her to bear with her nervous condition.

Holmes allowed her a moment to recover before resuming. "Jonathan Hawkins has been arrested, for both attempted murder and theft. I'm afraid he is not who he pretended to be. He is a criminal who works with the criminal underworld of London." He paused to let the words sink in.

Miss Baylor, at the very first words, had begun to sob into her handkerchief. I did all that I could to comfort her, but nothing could help the matter. I turned to Holmes, who was watching our guest with concern in his eyes. He said nothing.

~*~

Mrs. Hudson returned with the tea a quarter of an hour later. Miss Baylor had by then recovered some, but was still distressed. Holmes was leaning back in his chair with his eyes closed. Our landlady did not appear disturbed by the strange sight in our sitting room; she went around, pouring tea as if we were at a tea-party before seating herself beside Miss Baylor. No one spoke for some time. Miss Baylor pulled at the lace on her handkerchief absentmindedly, while Mrs. Hudson continuously added sugar cubes to Holmes' tea. I kept my eyes on Holmes, who never stirred or made a sound. It was most awkward.

"Holmes," I began, hoping for some acknowledgement of our company.

Holmes sat upright. "Ah, yes, Watson." He rubbed his hands together. "Is everyone enjoying their tea?"

This statement was so uncharacteristic of him that Mrs. Hudson and I began to laugh. I could see an amused smile play at the corners of Holmes' mouth. This lightened the mood somewhat. Then Holmes began to explain the events of the past few days. Everyone, especially Miss Baylor, listened intently.

~*~

"Three days ago, Mrs. Hudson entered the room at a very uncanny hour. She appeared quite perturbed. This note," he drew it out of his pocket, "was the cause of her distress.

"After interviewing Billy, I knew that something strange was going on; the commoner would not leave a note such as this one taped to a door. It is very vague, and would require its author to explain the contents in detail.

"The fact that the author of the note had printed it, and then left it attached to the door at such a strange hour, suggested to me that he was attempting remain unidentified. Upon closer examination of the note, it was discovered that the handwriting was heavy, suggesting that the author was, indeed, a man.

"I sent Watson to Hyde Park. He was approached by a strange, unknown man - tall, and of muscular build, with dark hair - who appeared to the commoner as a friendly acquaintance. Caught up in conversation, he forgot to ask the man his name. Watson was able to fully describe him to me. This helped in forming the connections. The man he described precisely fit the description of a certain Jonathan Hawkins, whom I knew to be involved with petty thefts in previous years. I had never acquired enough evidence to convict him, as he would lay low for awhile after each crime before returning to the trade. I decided not to take up the pointless task of trying to find him and his accomplices - there would not be any presentable evidence, which would prevent his arrest. I had previously returned with this box," he held it up, "after going about the city of London disguised as the original owner, wishing to retrieve it due to some family scandal over it. As you can see, I was able to recover the box. I spent some time examining it, before attempting to open it. According to Mrs. Hudson, the box appraised at worth nothing - not even a shilling."

I nodded approvingly and Holmes continued.

"Because of this information I was able to tentatively confirm my suspicions - the box, though believed it was worthless, was actually very valuable. I had not yet determined why, but, if Hawkins was after it, there must be something worth pursuing; perhaps inside the box. I was able to open the box after some time. The outside lock was unlike anything I've ever seen before; it required pressure on certain petals from each flower. Once opened, another set of locks under the lid prevented me from further investigation. I would have dispatched a telegram to you, Miss Baylor, except it would not have made it to Derbyshire Street until morning. By then I would have arrived. When I arrived at the Baylor's the butler informed me that the entire family was out, and would not be returning until the afternoon. This was somewhat disheartening, as it slowed down the investigation. I returned to Baker Street to find another note, this time warning Mrs. Hudson of danger if she did not follow the orders. This drew my attention. Mrs. Hudson would have to be kept under close supervision until the end of the investigation. It was then that I remembered an article I had glanced over in the 'Times' of a fortnight ago. Scotland Yard had made another attempt at finding the missing Crown Jewels of Scotland."

At this Miss Baylor and Mrs. Hudson both gasped.

"The crown jewels?" Miss Baylor cried.

Holmes nodded, then resumed. "The attempt was in vain, however. At this point I was beginning to speculate that the mind behind the plan was Moriarty - Hawkins was not intelligent enough to orchestrate the timing of the notes with the article on his own. It was a small article...

I agreed aloud. I had missed the article entirely.

"I wondered if he had somehow involved himself with Miss Baylor. Moriarty would have informed him of the family connections by then.

"Everything was confirmed when you arrived, Miss Baylor, at my orders. Your fiancé remained outdoors, while the interview was conducted."

My friend paused in his narrative. "Miss Baylor, Hawkins did not return with you to your house that day."

Miss Baylor confirmed this by shaking her head sadly. "I thought nothing of it. He would not climb back into the cab, insisting that he had some minor business to attend to - he would meet me at Barton's for dinner, he said."

Holmes folded his hands. "Of course. His business consisted of watching the flat, to catch Mrs. Hudson on the way out to perform any tasks. Before you left, you informed me of your Scottish heritage. You brought with you a journal, which, upon examination, revealed the combination for the second lock; by decoding a single entry, then solving an anagram, I was able to unlock the box. This, however, only resulted in a yellowed piece of parchment being revealed. I must admit this was slightly disappointing, but refused to become discouraged. I examined the parchment and found the message on it to be written in short hand, of which I know a little. I became distracted for a moment, translating the message. Watson, however, noticed that the proportions of the box were incorrect, and this led to his discovery of the second chamber. We opened it together, and I drew out the pouch, which, I had confirmed, contained the missing crown jewels."

I was more than pleased that Holmes has seen fit to attribute this discovery to me, especially as I was so rarely the recipient of Holmes' approbation.

"The pieces were fitting together nicely. A plan began to formulate; this would be the opportune time to catch a villain that has been roaming free for years, thieving and eluding capture. He was after the missing crown jewels, associating with Moriarty, and leaving threatening notes intended for our completely innocent landlady.

Unfortunately, Watson fell ill yesterday upon discovery of the jewels and became unconscious. I was not able to acquire his help to execute my plan. I had to make a few adjustments, and, leaving Watson at Baker Street, Mrs. Hudson and I walked to Hyde Park. I followed Mrs. Hudson at a discreet distance - anyone keeping their attention focused on the landlady with the gold-engraved box would not notice Sherlock Holmes strolling the walkways with his cane. I finally settled myself on a park bench several hundred feet away from Mrs. Hudson, in a small grove of willow trees which succeeded in hiding me from view. I watched as Mrs. Hudson placed the box under the bench and began walking back to Baker Street. I remained seated, intending to follow her to the flat to ensure her safety. It was then I noticed a strange man - not Hawkins - lurking in the shadows behind the tall elm tree. I glanced around without discovering any more hidden men, and dashed out of my hiding place, but it was too late; the man had taken Mrs. Hudson while I had diverted my attention. I had no idea where they had gone. I ran to the clearing, hoping for some clue as to which direction they had gone, but found none. As I paused to sort my thoughts, I heard the footfalls of someone approaching from behind. I turned just in time to see Hawkins, who, I must admit, appeared to have been expecting me."

"We exchanged words, and I, careful not to insult him, began to take leave of him. But he followed me, and when we had just passed the grove of willows he took hold of me and pulled me in. I must say that I am grateful for my previous days of boxing; without my knowledge on the subject I would surely be dead instead of sitting before you now. Hawkins left me in the grove. I was able to pull myself to the edge of the grove before I collapsed; it was rather exhausting to perform such a small task. I lay still for a few moments before Lestrade appeared on the footpath, conversing with a small number of his men. He saw me lying in the grove and came to my aid, helping me to the flat. Thus how I came to be back at Baker Street in the condition you found me, Watson. I informed them that Hawkins would surely arrive at the flat and inquire about the jewels, and that I would have you prepared to meet him. They were to come to the sitting room when they heard the sound of a pistol firing - I could only pray that it was mine that they would hear."

Before he could continue, I interrupted him. "Holmes, why did you not inform me that the police were here? It would have caused me much less pain if I would have known for sure we were to be rescued!"

Holmes shook his head. "I was afraid that if you knew, Watson, your act wouldn't be as convincing as it was. Hawkins believed you were alone, and I was therefore able to catch him red-handed trying to take the jewels from you. If your act wasn't convincing, it would have been much less efficient in catching him - highly improbable, actually. Everything went according to plan. Lestrade responded quickly to my shot, and Hawkins was caught with a gun to Watson's head - it all lined up perfectly for a convincing case of attempted murder. Mrs. Hudson was returned to us - she had been kept in the abandoned restaurant on Grosvenor Street - although her kidnapper was nowhere to be found."

Mrs. Hudson looked the most surprised out of the group. "And to think that all of this started with one little wedding-present!"

Holmes smiled. "That is the beauty of the case."

"Holmes," I began, "what will we do with the jewels? They are obviously property of the Royal Family."

"No, Watson, they are not," Holmes said. At my confused look he added, "The journal states, on page twenty-five I believe, that Queen Mary Stuart gave the jewels to her maid, Ailsa Todd, as a wedding gift before she was executed."

I understood then. "Then they rightfully belong to..."

Holmes nodded, and I returned the jewels to him."They rightfully belong to Miss Violet Baylor."

Miss Baylor covered her mouth with her hand, before reaching out to accept her treasure. "But I cannot..."

Holmes silenced her by putting a finger to his lips."You shall. They are yours, Miss Baylor. Part of your heritage."

"But I cannot take all of them! You played the game for me - you performed the dirty tasks, and the hunting and decoding; why, you even came near death in a battle not your own! You deserve to be paid, at least." She reached into the velvet pouch and removed a small, red ruby, about two centimeters across, and handed it to Holmes. "As payment, and a reminder of what a great service you have done to me and the country of Scotland."

Holmes hesitated for a moment before he took the ruby gently and held it up to the light, examining it thoroughly. His emotions took over for a moment, and he wasn't able to speak. He recovered quickly, however, to say, "Thank you, Miss Baylor."

Then Miss Baylor reached in again and pulled out two small diamonds and passed one to me. I thanked her heartily and put it in my pocket. She also handed one to Mrs. Hudson, but Mrs. Hudson refused.

"No, dear, I won't take one. I've had enough trouble with this box and jewel business as it is. You keep it."

Miss Baylor then embraced Mrs. Hudson, who appeared much moved. Then she turned to me, and shook my hand gently, whispering a small 'thank you' into my ear. I rose to show her out.

Holmes also rose, despite his injuries, and shook Miss Baylor's hand. "A pleasure to work with you, Miss Baylor," he said. "And thank you."

Miss Baylor was surprised. "For what, might I ask?"

We moved toward the door, and Holmes laughed. "For relieving me of my monotonous life," he said.

Mrs. Hudson showed our guest to the door, and Holmes silently retreated to his bedroom, examining the ruby all the way.

I myself situated myself on the settee, inspecting my own gem. While looking it over, I heard Holmes begin to play one of my favorite violin concertos. I leaned back, listening, all the while silently pondering the adventure of the gold-engraved box.

The Night Before Christmas~Mike B

'Twas the night before Christmas, and all through the house

Not a creature was stirring, not even a mouse.

The windows and doors were all fastened with care

For fear that a visitor soon would be there.

The children were all hiding under their beds

While visions of criminals danced in their heads.

And mamma in her 'kerchief, and I in my cap,

Were huddled together when we heard a tap.

Then out on the lawn there arose such a clatter,

I sprang from my chair to see what was the matter.

Away to the window I flew like a flash,

Tore open the shutters and threw up the sash.

The moon on the breast of the new-fallen snow

Gave the lustre of mid-day to objects below,

When, what to my wondering eyes should appear,

But a figure all sullen and sallow and sere.

Then I with a breath in a voice loud and hearty,

Let out a shrill cry, 'Great Scott, Moriarty!'

More rapid than eagles more villains then came,

And he whistled, and shouted, and called them by name;

"Now, Roylott! now, Slaney! now Dixie, and all!

On, Brunton! on, Howells! on, Jonathan Small!

To the top of the porch! to the top of the wall!

Now dash away! crash away! take away all!"

And mamma and I were a feared we were gone,

When they met with an obstacle out on the lawn,

So up to the door now the villains they flew,

But, Behold!, in an instant their plans were all through!

For then, in a twinkling, I heard on the roof

A sound giving all of my silent prayers proof -

As I drew back my head, and was turning around,

Down the chimney came Sherlock and in with a bound!

He was dressed all in tweed, from his head to his foot,

And his clothes were all tarnished with ashes and soot;

The children had come out from under the bed

And laughed at the deerstalker cap on his head.

His eyes -- how they twinkled! his dimples, how merry!

His nose like a hawk-bill, his chiselled chin, very!

His grinning wide mouth was drawn-up like a bow,

And what's that I see? well, what do you know -

A Calabash pipe he held tight in his teeth,

And the smoke it encircled his head like a wreath;

He had a thin face and a right regal bearing,

That spoke of a one who was fearless and daring.

He was figured and fit, a right jolly good chap,

And I smiled when I saw him, in spite of the cap!

A wink of his eye and a twist of his head,

Soon gave me to know I had nothing to dread;

He spoke not a word, but went right to his work,

And he straightened his cape, and then turned with a jerk,

And laying his finger aside of his nose,

And giving a nod, up the chimney he rose;

He sprang from the roof and then onto the lawn

And straightaway all of the villains were gone!

He gave a great shout and he gave a loud a whistle

And away they all flew like the down of a thistle.

But I heard him exclaim, as he drove them from sight,

Merry Christmas to all, and to all a good night!

Replacements~Paula Trott

It was the one and only time I had ever seen my friend look truly, achingly devastated. Another case had been concluded successfully, I recall, on that frosty night in early December. It had been a truly exhausting time for both Sherlock Holmes and me – my friend had been engaged by a young man in his early twenties not two days before, who had pleaded with Holmes to look into the deaths of his employer and a colleague. Both suicides - or so it would seem. The world's only consulting detective had, of course, reeled off a list of contradictions to this theory upon arrival at the crime scene, starting with the traces of gunpowder on the door-handle and ending with some oddly positioned bloodstains on the victims' suits. ("Observe their hands – clean, not a speck of blood on them. The only way the underarms of the suit jacket could have become bloodied is if a second person was here, and moved the body after death to suggest suicide. Pah! Child's play, Lestrade!")

As it turns out, the unfortunate gentlemen had been the victims of a desperate businessman who had become massively indebted to the company, and went to extremes to ensure he would not have to pay up. Unsurprisingly this fellow moved in disreputable circles, and it did not take long for news of Holmes' efforts to reach his ears. Shortly before his arrest, he, along with a gang of his ruffian friends, broke into our rooms at Baker Street and turned the place upside down. Our possessions were treated as steak thrown to lions. This little escapade was their downfall, however – they left enough mud on the carpet, along with snatches of clothing ripped and torn in the chaos, to lead Holmes right to them.

There were many casualties to be dealt with after the vile men had swept through our humble quarters with a ferocity which quite chilled me to the bone. Mrs. Hudson's beautiful Ming vase, a gift from her late husband, was one of the most significant – the poor woman was beside herself with fright and shock as it was and this, I fear, nearly broke her poor heart. The contents of my medical bag were mostly damaged beyond repair, to my outrage. It was not I who would suffer most from this; it was any poor creature (let alone Holmes or I) who needed my help before I had time to purchase replacements. How anyone could be so cold of heart was beyond me!

However, the damage was done, and it was no use allowing the anger I felt at those blackguards (whom, after all, were spending the night and probably many more in a grimy police cell) to take over. I took a deep breath and tried my very best to retain a high spirit in spite of the devastation - I resorted to allowing myself to be quietly amused by the sight of Holmes attempting to clear up... A task which, I can confidently reveal, he has had very little practice of. I knew from the look in his eyes that he had felt some guilt upon witnessing the state of Mrs. Hudson's nerves. Despite his occasional show of hostility towards our dear housekeeper, there was no denying that he was desperately grateful (as was I) to her for her seemingly never-ending patience. Holmes was picking his way haphazardly back and forth through the debris, accompanied by his ever-moving pile of odds and ends that flitted from the armchair, to his chemical table, to my desk, to the sofa, to the floor, and back to the armchair. Each item had been picked up and studied with a sense of having never seen it before in his life, his dark eyes glinting in the firelight. It was clear that he didn't quite know what to do with these funny little trivialities one acquires over time, his great brain probably working on too high a level to appreciate that sort of thing... Of course it would eventually fall to me to sort it all out again, but with a stifled chuckle and a shake of my head, I let him get on with it.

We worked on in silence, punctuated only by the rustle of paper, the occasional chink of broken glass and our own footsteps as we danced among the carnage, trying not to cause further damage. We must have looked quite ridiculous, dishevelled as we were, springing about our living room on tip-toes. However, I was too exhausted by the days' ventures to care very much and Holmes was no doubt still caught up in the thrill of the chase and subsequent capture of the villains. I too began to find myself lost in my own thoughts, losing awareness of what I was doing... and failing to realise that my companion had stopped moving.

I have developed an acute sense of awareness when it comes to something being wrong, which I can only attribute to my dealings in Holmes' cases. I felt the disturbingly familiar creeping sensation upon the back of my neck like some silent and deadly arachnid – I let the papers I was holding slide from my hands and turned.

Holmes was kneeling by the table in the corner, his dark hair dusted with cobwebs as if he had been crawling around underneath it. His back was turned towards me, but I could just make out the splintered, battered remains of his violin cradled in his pale, limp hands.

The curve of his spine, the tilt of his head, and the slight tremble of his fingers as he ran them disbelievingly over the snapped strings exhumed a grief I had not thought him capable of. I was frozen where I stood – it was a disturbing and pitiful sight to see. The brutal way in which the instrument had been destroyed made the blood run cold in my veins. As for its owner, he could have been a different man from the one I had not hours ago seen racing along the streets of London, spying tiny things with his eagle eyes that the rest of us had missed. Overcome with helplessness, I could do nothing but hastily retreat to my room – the moment he sensed my movement his fists clenched, the spine straightened a little as his own barriers slammed shut around him. I hesitated for a moment in the doorway... He set the pitiful collection of splinters down on the rug and swept away to his own bedroom, his face so expressionless and sharp it could have been carved from stone. I would get nothing out of him tonight.

~~~

The living room was lifeless when I came down for breakfast the next day. Taking in the grate full of discarded cigarette ends, still simmering softly amid the still-warm coals, I noted that Holmes had returned to the living room after my departure and could not have actually retired all that long ago. My breath hitched in my chest as I caught sight of the broken violin laid out as if in state on the sofa, skeletal remains and strings neatly arranged. The bow, I noticed with a pang, was arranged beside it in a similar fashion, a jagged break in the middle where it had been snapped in two. I sighed, the smell of bacon and eggs assaulting my senses. The tortured instrument leered up at me. I wasn't hungry.

What could I do? The curse of being a medical man, I'm afraid...the need to find a solution, to mend what has been broken, or to at least go as far as I can to ease suffering. I wandered over to the coal scuttle and helped myself to one of the remaining cigars. Neither of us could afford to replace the violin completely, and I knew my friend's pride would cause him to dismiss the idea of going halves before the words had left my lips. So... What was to be done? I chose that moment, fortunately, to slip my hand into my pocket. As my hand clenched around the crumpled and unanswered telegram within, a wave of relief swept over me. I had...potentially...an answer.

~~~

Holmes was still locked away in his room when I returned from the post office, and there were still no signs of life by the time my message had received a reply. This seclusion was further proof that the destruction of his beloved instrument had hit him hard, and I was anxious that the rest of the day should run as smoothly as possible. I knew a cab was coming to collect us at three o'clock...forty five minutes.

Obstacle number one: extricating the world's only

75

consulting detective from his room. Easy to say, harder to do. I considered the good old knock-and-shout method, but experience had taught me I would most likely get naught but verbal abuse for my efforts. I reconsidered.

I have to say, it was worth the embarrassment of having Holmes open the door on me trying and failing (miserably) to pick his lock to hear him give a little snort of amusement, and see the faintest twitch of a smile sweep across his features.

"It's a fine art, Watson." He sighed as he stepped over my cringing form. His voice was low and grating, and the energy and vigour I had witnessed not twenty four hours ago had vanished from his stride, which was now more of a shuffle. It looked somewhat bizarre to see his long legs actually dragging his feet on the floor – the situation was much worse than I had first supposed. I wondered, as I stood up and took in his pale face and dark-ringed eyes, whether he had slept at all. I went straight to the point as he crumpled into his armchair, wriggling his feet out of his scuffed slippers.

"A cab is to be sent to our door in half an hour, Holmes. Your brother needs your assistance." My companion's eyes snapped up to me in surprise (or as close to surprise as Sherlock Holmes was ever likely to get) from their despondent gaze at the sofa.

"Mycroft?" I could practically see the images of national scandal racing through his mind as he puffed his one surviving pipe into life.

"Hmm." I confirmed vaguely, unable to meet his eye as I settled down at the table and helped myself to some cold bacon. I felt a little guilty as he leapt up from his chair, vaulted over the sofa and dashed back to his room to make himself look presentable, pipe ash flying all over the place. "Lord God," I murmured to myself as I briefly abandoned my breakfast to smother a stray bit of ash which was threatening to set our rug alight, "Let him be as enthused by the truth as he is by the lie!"

~~~

Of course, the cab ride was terribly awkward. Fifteen solid minutes of interrogation upon the matter of a crime, suspects, and "Facts, Watson, facts!" that simply did not exist conducted by a bloodhound eager for a scent was exhausting. By the time we pulled up at the music shop, Holmes was calling me all sorts of unbecoming names because I had "forgotten" to bring the telegram with me for him to study. Unfortunately, showing him would mean the element of surprise in our true cause would be lost completely, so I forced an apologetic smile and agreed that my brain was "so full of twaddle from that romantic rubbish you read I'm surprised you are still able to dress yourself" and, with a sigh, reminded myself that he probably hadn't slept very much last night.

Not a moment too soon, the cab bounced to a halt, the horses' hooves clattering upon the cobbled streets with finality. There were clouds overhead and the air had become clouded with gentle snowfall, but I was still able to make out the portly figure of Mycroft Holmes through the shop window, deep in conversation with the owner. I watched from the corner of my eye as his younger brother froze in his seat, eyes darting from the fading treble clef above the weather-beaten shop door, to his sibling inside, to me. I took a deep breath and turned to him.

"We're here." It was all I could think of to say. There was no doubt that he had now cottoned on. His lips thinned, the little crease in the centre of his forehead deepened – I must say that for a moment, a silent panic gripped me. I am certainly not afraid of Sherlock Holmes, but it did (and still does) unsettle me that, having known each other for so long, I find him so difficult to read sometimes. He realised his eyes were giving him away, so he turned his glare to the floor of the carriage. Withdrawing from the living, feeling world. Curling up into a ball of spikes, like a defensive hedgehog, not letting anyone near. By God, the man was brilliant, but damned frustrating!

"Watson," he began. I could tell, just by the way he said my name, that one word, that he did not mean what he was about to say. It was as if he was reading from an over-rehearsed script. "It does not matter. In any case, I really...cannot afford..."

"That doesn't come into it, Holmes." I interrupted. The eyes – flickering up to the window – out of his control. I was winning. He played his last card...

"I will not be reduced to begging..." he cocked an eyebrow at his elder brother who, I observed as I followed Holmes' gaze, was now waving us in with a meaty hand. This charade had gone on for long enough, I decided.

"Of course not," I grumbled, sliding out of the cab and giving him my very best look of exasperation. "Begging requires the asking for something and since you have done no such thing, you are not begging." He didn't move. I leaned into the cab again. "Holmes...come on, old fellow. At least come into the warm and have a look?" How ironic. Now *I* was doing the begging. Thankfully, my companion made up his mind to humour me, and dropped from the carriage with cat-like grace.

Mycroft Holmes gave us an unexpectedly (but by no means unwelcome) warm greeting, vigorously shaking my hand and clapping his brother on the shoulder.

"Dr. Watson...Sherlock, my boy, come inside. Doctor, I see you were successful in your flutter at the races last week, congratulations." Beside me, the younger Holmes gave an indignant "Hmm!" And shot me a glare that could melt iron. Damn it, it was just the once, and I had taken such precautions against Holmes finding out! I quelled further negative thoughts as the shop keeper, a jovial-looking middle-aged man with rosy cheeks, was introduced to us. I would no doubt get the gambling lecture later, back in Baker Street, but I had taken to counteracting it with a few choice arguments regarding my friend's use of cocaine. It is rather pleasant to win in a disagreement with Sherlock Holmes, once in a while. Lord knows, it doesn't happen very often.

What followed was...odd. As most things are when dealing with Holmes's. I almost felt like an intruder – the brothers stood face-to-face, both looking decidedly uncomfortable. One of them had sent a telegram to his sibling's closest and only friend admitting he hadn't a clue what to give to his brother as a Christmas gift. The other was agonisingly torn between his own swollen pride and...well, emotion.

So it was heart-warming and, I admit, a great comfort to me to see Mycroft take my friend by his slender shoulders and steer him in the direction of the back of the shop. I followed, timidly, and found myself in an area packed out with hundreds of the most exquisitely crafted violins I have ever seen in my life. The smell of varnished wood and rosin was glorious. The way the candle light played across the maple and spruce wood and gave the ebony a deep, burning glow was hypnotic. In that moment I envied my friend's great musical talent, the ability to make such a beautiful thing sing. He was wearing an expression similar to the one he reserves for our trips to the concert-hall...absolute rapture.

"Have a good look, Sherlock," croaked the elder Holmes, with a softness that caught me off guard. His hands were still on his brother's shoulders. With a stab of bittersweet nostalgia I was reminded of the comradeship I had once shared with my own brother as a child. Faded memories flashed across my vision – carols around the Christmas tree and battles with toy soldiers...another world. I slipped my hand into my pocket and closed my fingers around the ancient pocket-watch within, as Mycroft continued. "Take your time. Mr. Dunstan will help you, should you require assistance – and do not even think of asking after a price. I'm sure the good Doctor and I can entertain ourselves sufficiently." With a jolt, I pulled myself together, smiled encouragingly at Holmes, and followed Mycroft out of the shop.

And so it was I found myself sat in a tea room with the other Holmes. To my great surprise, the time we spent together was not as awkward as I had first supposed. Mycroft Holmes sat before me like some larger-than-life stuffed animal, greying hair perfectly groomed and clothes starched and spotless. The bright, mischievous eyes he shared with his brother were darting here, there and everywhere... The sight of subconscious deduction was oddly reassuring.

"You know," he had stated in his low, rumbling tone when the conversation turned to the loss of Holmes' beloved instrument, "It surprises me a little that you know of his skill as a violinist at all. Sherlock never performed for anyone, not even our... relatives..." I sipped my tea. There was something distinctly unpleasant and forced about the way he referred to the rest of the illusive Holmes clan. I didn't press it.

"I wouldn't call them...performances, as such," said I, recalling being woken many times during the night to what sounded like a cat being slowly squashed.

"But when he does play properly, it really is wonderful...I hear it quite by accident, most of the time."

"Ah..." replied Mycroft, his wide, frog-like mouth curving upwards slightly, "Still torturing the thing to aid concentration, is he?" I had to laugh. And feel a not a little relieved that I was clearly not the only one to be subjected to that awful racket.

"Sometimes, yes. But, as I say, when he does play...proper music...his talent is quite astounding. "

Mycroft's smile grew wider, eyes gleaming. I wondered idly what Sherlock would be like, seven years on...would he be more at ease with himself, as his brother seemed to be? It had occurred to me, on more than one occasion, that the great intelligence with which my friend was endowed was both a blessing and a curse. A brain with such great power, leagues ahead of all others...It frustrated him terribly, having to wait for the rest of the world to catch up. Holmes had maintained from the outset that Mycroft's mental abilities were greater than his own, and yet...here was Mycroft, making simple conversation with someone whose mind could not be more different than his own. Was it age? Was it experience? Was it the difference in energy and ambition? I could not be sure. My brother's pocket watch seemed to burn at my side.

"Our mother taught us," My enigmatic companion continued. "I'm sure Sherlock has given you his 'Art in the blood' speech – she was as passionate for her music as it was possible to be."

"She taught you also? The violin?"
He drained his cup of tea, and I did likewise, relishing the taste. Mycroft donned his top hat.

"The Cello."

~~~

Upon our return, Sherlock Holmes was standing at the oaken counter, lips twitching as they so often did when he struggled to keep from smiling. His brand new violin was being carefully packed into a box by an ever-smiling Mr. Dunstan, who passed my friend his gift as we approached. Holmes' eyes blazed. It was as if he had been handed a pot of gold.

"I trust my colleague has...ah..." Mr. Dunstan flashed Mycroft a smile.

"All taken care of, sir!" He declared. Colour flushed vividly in my friend's pale, hollow cheeks for a moment. We said our cheery goodbyes and thank-you, and stepped back out into the snowy street.

The sky was beginning to darken. I took a couple of steps away from the siblings. "Thank you, Mycroft." I could just hear Holmes mutter. The words sounded foreign on his lips.

"I have said it before, and I shall say it again, Sherlock," replied Mycroft as he eased his large frame into a waiting cab, "We are not brothers for nothing." He winked a beady eye at me, shut the door, and in a flurry of snowflakes and the clop of horses' hooves, he was gone.

~~~

Back at Baker Street – looking spick and span once more, thanks to the efforts of our truly indispensable housekeeper – Holmes was finally able to unpack his gift. Silently he placed the instrument under his chin, his long, thin fingers getting used to the feel of the new strings. He said nothing as he raised the bow... but looked over to me, curled up in my arm chair...and *beamed*. It was the widest, most joyful smile I had ever witnessed, and it was genuine.

I closed my eyes and, for the first time since my return home from Afghanistan all that time ago, felt completely and utterly at peace as the first notes of my favourite carol unfurled, rich and beautiful, into the air...

Silent night,
Holy night.
All is calm,
All is bright.
'Round yon virgin, mother and child,
Holy infant, so tender and mild.
Sleep in Heavenly peace...
Sleep in Heavenly peace.

The Shapeshifter~Cassie Parkes

Blood spots splatter his face,

He doesn't care, he loves the chase!

But run away from his sweeping embrace,

He only wants you for his newest case!

Beware his trail, he's always in front.

Don't speak to him; he's harsh, true and blunt.

His only friend is a doctor, I'm told.

How can he defend a man who's so cold?

He dreams not of glories, but of justice and death.

Most of his friends have seen their last breath.

Not a Grim Reaper, nor a God, or a priest.

Some call him a hero; others say he's a beast.

The Magic of Music~David Rowbotham

It was New Years Day 1886, an animated Holmes was reading excitedly from the latest edition of the Illustrated London News.

"Here it is Watson, The Metropolitan Tramroad Company have announced that they are to commence testing of their electric mechanical tramcars. These most modern of conveyances are moved along the track by means of large motors with power supplied from lead acid accumulator batteries. This is progress indeed! And they are to test them upon the route from the Marylebone Road to Regents Park which runs right past here along Baker Street. This will be a sight to see"

"Well, I think it's a great shame Holmes, in my opinion these contraptions are the most unnatural of devices to meet in the street. The street is the proper place for living creatures, for people and horses and for horse drawn conveyances. These mechanical monsters should be confined to their own courses in the same way in which the locomotives of the railways are confined to their own tracks and not mixed in with the public pedestrian. I have recently seen one of these horseless electric cars in Westminster, it made a most curious whining and wailing noise as it proceeded along its track."

"Ah, it would seem that they recognise your concern Watson, they do assure the News that they will only operate during daylight so as not to cause undue alarm to any who encounter the scene"

"Nevertheless, Holmes, I cannot say I share your

enthusiasm for progress on this occasion, to put our future in the hands of inventors and crackpots is most foolhardy I feel." I could see that this was an area we would not come to consensus upon, then I remembered my earlier encounter with Mrs. Hudson.

"Ah, Holmes, I nearly forgot, Mrs. Hudson gave me this for you, it was hand delivered earlier today." I took a small envelope addressed to 'Mr. Sherlock Holmes' out of my pocket and handed it to him. He examined the envelope for a full minute or more before proceeding to open it. Inside was a small visitor's card.

"What is it, Holmes?"

"It's……… erm, it's…………….. it, it is nothing Watson, nothing whatsoever!" He slipped the card hurriedly into his waistcoat pocket, and proceeded to pace around the room in a most irritated fashion. He then began repeatedly taking out, reading and then re-pocketing the card for the next few hours.

Holmes paused from his pent up perambulations to pick up his violin which he then thrust most fiercely under his chin.

"My bow, Watson?"

I looked around. "I would presume that it is precisely where you left it, Holmes"

"Yes, and where was that?"

"Well, how should I know?"

"You should observe Watson, my good man, you should pay attention. It's all in the detail"

"You mean you've lost it, Holmes………" I smiled.

"Ah, here it is. See, details; details!"

His bow was thrust well into the soil of the Aspidistra which grew slumberingly from its pot on the plant stand in the window. I'm sure it was doing the bow no good at all. Holmes retrieved his bow and resuming his pose he lifted the soil encrusted bow to the strings. As he postured to strike his first blow I squeezed my eyes shut and braced myself against the imminent howl of protest about to erupt from his oft tortured instrument.

Silence….

I held my breath and waited……….

Silence…

I opened first one eye……. and then the other.

Holmes was frozen. Mid-thought. The next instant his
violin was back against the wall besides the fireplace.
"On guard!" he cried, and proceeded to dance maniacally
around the room, left arm dangling limply over his head like a
demented ape, fencing some imaginary opponent. This went on
for a full five minutes before Holmes slumped into his chair.
"Silence man! I need to think…."
Holmes did not utter another word that night, he just sat
staring into the space between us, as though waiting for someone
to materialise there. I took myself off to my room for an early
night leaving Holmes to contemplate the meaning of his visitor's
card.
I was up early the next morning as I had patients at my
surgery to attend to, but Holmes had already risen and left 221B.
Clearly he had something on his mind, but I thought nothing more
of it, he knew where I would be and he could send a runner to my
surgery should he need to get hold of me.
I returned to 221B late that afternoon to find a note on
Holmes desk *'Watson, I have some little task which is requiring of
my attention. I shall see you in a few days. S.H.'* A few quiet
evenings at our lodgings would not go amiss, it would mean I
could catch up on my notes and talk to my publisher about my
next instalments.
I was awoken that night by the most blood curdling of
animal noises coming from below my room. A sound not unlike
that of foxes mating, counterpoised by a whole street of mongrel
tomcats at war. It fair made the hairs stand up upon my neck. On
and on it seemed to go, on and on without end. Then it ceased,
just as quickly as it had started and eventually I was able to regain
my sleep. The following day followed the same pattern as the

previous one. Night time arrived with monotonous certainty and I had but briefly attained a deepness of sleep when once again I was brought rudely to a state of wakefulness by a most unholy row. This time it sounded as though one of the Metropolitan Tramroad Company electric cars had managed to entangle a family of cats amongst its various workings whilst traversing the length of Baker Street because there followed a most inhuman squealing and howling which I can only hope was not generated of some human source, but was indeed entirely mechanical, so extreme and excruciating was its clamour. Thankfully as with the previous night, the noises abated as quickly as they had started.

The next day there was still no sign of Holmes, although Mrs. Hudson did tell me that he had been up to our lodgings during the day and she had seen him carrying his violin and bow with a notable degree of intent. Such behaviour to me seemed somewhat unusual, that beloved instrument of his rarely being seen outside the confines of our drawing room.

Well, on the third night since the disappearance of Holmes, the intrusion of the noises occurred once again, seemingly within minutes of my head caressing my pillow, this time it was not unlike a pack of dogs serenading someone dragging their nails down a blackboard. Delightful! What was going on? I wondered….

That morning as I was leaving I bumped into Mrs, Hudson; I asked her if she had been disturbed by the noises in the night but she did not hear me at first.

"I'm sorry Dr Watson; what was that you were saying? Oh, please wait a moment, I've still got my ear plugs in………." She did not need to say any more, it was clear that she'd heard nothing, I resolved to follow her example in the ensuing nights and indeed that next night I was not troubled by any noise whatsoever and went off to my surgery in a much lighter frame of mind, no doubt much to the benefit of my grateful patients…….

I arrived back at 221B on the evening of the 5th to find Mrs. Hudson in a most agitated state.

"Well, she marches in here as bold as you please.'I'm expected.' She said. 'I'll show myself in.' She insisted. Dr Watson,

I could not stop her"

"Who, Mrs Hudson?"

"Why, that bawdy Vaudeville monologist, that's who!"

"Oh, I see"

I shook my head, none the wiser I set off up the stairs to our lodgings to determine the identity of this mystery visitor.

"Ah, Doctor Watson, what a pleasure" The acid in her voice was burning in my ears almost before she had spoken, clearly her words did not match her feelings., neither did they match her appearance for I would say her appearance was matchless, the very pinnacle of her sex.

"The feeling is mutual, I'm sure" I smiled awkwardly, obviously I was not who she was waiting for, and yet clearly she knew of me, but I had no idea of the identity of this strange, forthright and most beautiful of women. Quite the fairest vista my eyes had feasted upon in an assuredly long time. I assume she had read my published reports of Holmes escapades, and it was clear she was not going to indulge me the intent behind her visit.

"Erm, Mr Holmes is not here at the moment" I said, fumbling for somewhere to place my hands. I clasped the back of the chair at Holmes writing desk. The young woman before me wore a delicate silver locket which hung from the finest of silver chains adorning her neck. Captivated I followed the line of the chain from her neck down to…. to where the locket nestled. Suddenly realising she was watching me with intent bemusement, I drew my gaze back to her wondrously deep almond eyes and waited, hopefully not open mouthed…..I closed my mouth.

"So I see, that's alright, I shall wait. He is expecting me."

"In the meantime would you be so kind as to unlock the lid on your piano"

"Hmmm, well I do not see why not."

I busied myself looking for the key glad of the distraction from this most distracting of attractiveness. The key would, or rather it should, be in the deeper recesses of Holmes desk drawer. It was so rare that the piano was unlocked; indeed except for the annual visit from Mr Rogersan Hammersteinway, the blind piano tuner, I don't think its keys ever struck a note. Certainly I'd never heard it played in anger, unlike Holmes' violin which only ever seemed to be played in anger.

"A problem Doctor?"

The visitor was right behind me as I rummaged through Holmes desk, making me feel distinctly uncomfortable and taking far more of an interest in the drawer contents than I cared for.

"No, here it is" Relieved, my fingers had at last found the small brass key which permitted access to the ivories. I unlocked the lid and raised it with a hand which shook too much to not be noticed, clearly much to the satisfaction of the visitor, as she brusquely elbowed past me to take up a position on the small stool. She ran a white gloved hand gently, caressingly, over the keys. I found I was holding my breath.

"Ah, what a delightful pianino!" She exclaimed, "I've not found myself seated before such an exquisite instrument in many years." "I am surprised; I did not expect to find such a masterpiece in your humble lodgings. This is excellent and so much more than I had anticipated."

She melted visibly. I swallowed before I spoke, "I can send a runner for Mr Holmes if you are in a hurry" I suggested. "If you can give me your name I shall get right on it"

She smiled; I had been thwarted in my attempt to learn this beautiful creature's name.

"Ah Dr Watson, I intrigue you, truly you do not know me? Your housekeeper recognised me straight away, I am disappointed in you sir, I had expected more from such a friend and colleague of the great Sherlock Holmes."

"Mrs. Hudson is not our housekeeper, she is our landlady and I apologise if my ignorance of you gives you offence. I'm sure I would remember you if our paths had crossed before."

"It's alright, Watson," Sherlock Holmes had walked into the room unnoticed. I never cease to marvel at how Holmes does that. "I see you two have made one another's acquaintance."

"Miss. Adler, it is good to meet you at last, do you have the necessary…"

"Ah Dr. Watson here was good enough to unlock"

"You're Adler!" "The Irene Adler, late of the Imperial

Opera of Warsaw?"

"Indeed, my good Doctor, I am the late Irene Adler...."
She smiled a far too knowing smile; I suspect I may have blushed.

Holmes was standing in the middle of the room, his violin held by its neck in his left hand hung limply at his side, he scratched his right ear with his bow looking deep in thought.

"Dr Watson, If you will excuse us" He raised his eyebrows and nodded his head very slightly in the direction of my room.

"I'm sorry, Holmes.... Oh; yes; err, of course."

I bowed curtly to our adorable visitor and winked at Holmes before backing into my room,

"An early night I think is in order, I'll bid you both goodnight."

I nodded a last bow as I turned into my room, closing the door quietly behind me. I'm not used to being dismissed by Holmes when we have a professional visit, so I can only assume that this evening was otherwise. I did not hear a single word spoken between those two unique characters alone in the Drawing room but I can tell you that they certainly made the magical music that evening. As I lay on my bed, it became clear to me what had been happening in the days since I had last seen Holmes; he had been practicing his mastery of that blessed instrument of his, and practicing hard. I could not help but hear the results of his secret endeavours as I lay there in the darkness.

I do not remember falling asleep, but sleep I did. When I arose that next morning our guest was long gone. Holmes never made mention of what transpired that night, and I respected my friend too much to ever raise the subject myself. All I know is that Holmes was never quite the same again after that meeting.

Cold~Jane Stuart

I'm a vengeful Victorian lady;

My husband, alas, is in jail.

It was Holmes who had made sure

His crimes were all paid for;

And our schemes to make money would fail.

~0~

I constantly think of my husband;

Alone, in his bleak prison cell.

For fifteen long years

I have shed many tears

For my spouse (and that money, as well.)

~0~

To add to my sense of injustice;

My name was in print; I had heard.

In "The Strand" was a page

Which suffused me with rage.

"Abominable"; just one word!

~o~

I am not really one to hold grudges;

But I think that detective should pay.

Revenge, I am told,

Is a dish best served cold;

He'll be sorry he got in my way!

~0~

I have studied his habits and movements;

Made notes on each foible and whim.

I have learned all I can

Of the heart of this man,

And what actions might devastate him.

~0~

I could burn down his Baker Street lodgings;

He wouldn't be happy with that.

I could slander his mother,

Or blackmail his brother,

Or murder his landlady's cat.

~0~

Or, of course, there's his loyal companion.

A kidnap; a ransom demand!

He might even pay double,

With Watson in trouble.

(And I haven't forgotten "The Strand")

~0~

If, by chance, Holmes refused to oblige me;

My response would be chillingly clear.

I'd announce my ambition

To kill a physician;

And Watson would just disappear.

~0~

This would not be too hard to accomplish;

I know what could act as my bait.

I could simply pretend

I was nearing the end;

Send a note to his clinic...and wait.

~0~

When he rushed to my aid, I'd be ready,

With gun, ether, shackles and key.

I would make Holmes regret he

Had crossed Ricoletti,

And regret he had ever crossed me!

~0~

later...

I penned my sad plea for assistance;

A boy, passing by, took my note.

As I sounded so sickly;

I was sure he'd come quickly;

Once he'd read every word that I wrote.

~o~

I waited, and peered through the window;

How could he resist my sad plight?

A ragged old crone;

Wandered past on her own;

Glanced my way, and then moved out of sight.

~0~

Two labourers slouched in a doorway,

Three boys played a game at their feet;

Then I smiled at the sound

Made by hooves on the ground.

As a carriage appeared in the street.

~0~

The doctor approached, as expected,

And knocked on my shabby front door.

I was ready, as planned;

Gun and ether in hand;

He stepped in, after knocking once more.

~0~

I stood with my cloth at the ready;

My moment of triumph, at last!

As he checked out the room,

I moved close, in the gloom...

Then the scene changed incredibly fast!

~0~

The doctor turned swiftly towards me;

I was gripped by two arms like a vice.

That ragged old crone,

In a soft, steel-edged tone,

Whispered," Drop it; I won't ask you twice."

~0~

I knew, straight away, I was beaten;

My plans for the future were shattered.

They'd ruined my fun;

I threw down my gun,

By the side of Holmes' skirts, where it clattered.

~0~

Holmes took off his flower trimmed bonnet,

His features were cold, grim and hard.

"This is how it must end

If you threaten my friend"

Then he called in two men from "The Yard".

~0~

later...

Tomorrow, I'm at the Old Bailey,

For the harm to the doctor I'd planned.

I am sure I'll do time

For my terrible crime,

But, I've earned some more lines in "The Strand".

Trick Or Treat~Mike B

      As we all know, at certain times of the year, even the most assiduous and involved of us - such as my good friend, Mr. Sherlock Holmes - are unashamedly drawn into the spirit of the season, whether it be on account of comfortable childhood memories or merely as a time to gather our own thoughts and reflect on the general course of things up to that time.

      I had received a telegram from Holmes on Oct.30th asking me to stop by the next day and to bring some of my notes from an unfinished account of one of our older adventures together, and I had this with me when I started out just at dusk on the 31st.

      And I have been invited to this address countless times and we have been interrupted repeatedly throughout the years by various persons in various states of distress and alarm, many of which required and received immediate action regardless of our other plans. But I must say, even so, when I arrived at the familiar environs of 221B, I was greeted by and became involved in the most absurd spectacle I believe it has ever been my embarrassment to have to commit to record.

      I left my cab and walked up to the door, and after knocking for some time and not getting a response, I became a bit wary, but then I heard a most odd muffled command coming from within -

      "The key's in the planter!"

      I looked over and there was a small packet left under the bougainvillea leaves and I retrieved it, unravelled it and found the key and this rather ominous note:

"Abandon all hope ye who enter herein"

I had begun to get uneasy, but Holmes had not let on as to any immediate threat to his safety recently, so I let myself in and was greeted by something that I have still not fully recovered from. I wasn't sure at first, but there was what appeared to be a lady of royalty of some sort facing away from me as I exited the foyer and started towards the living room area.. . . and then, shockingly, this person suddenly wheeled around and it was none other than Holmes himself!

"*Voilá*, Watson! I am trying out my new line of designer disguises early this year, and I'm sure that this will go well in London, as long as I can get it in enough shades and sizes -"what do you think?"

As I struggled to catch my breath, I wasn't quite sure what he was talking of, but then I knew enough also to never question the motives or seemingly odd ways of this man; but on seeing this, I could hardly do anything more than bleat out the following phrase;

"But really Holmes, *the Queen?!?!* What on earth has got into you, man?"

But before this had time to completely ruin my sight, I was then assaulted by a perhaps an even more shocking vision: Mrs. Hudson - wearing a bowler hat, a huge false moustache, yellow trousers, and a loud green vest with the most preposterous pink scarf around her neck, and a pair of old scuffed-up riding boots - came from the kitchen area carrying a tea tray with a number of cups on it upside down. She was coming from behind me and had I turned to address her.

"And just who are you supposed to be, Mrs Hudson?" I asked, somewhat gingerly.

"Why, the Prime Minister, of course! The table is all made up and ready for you, Dr. Watson. . ."

I looked over towards the dining room, and indeed, she had the whole table inexplicably made up for nine guests. I stood numb for what seemed an eternity, and then gathered myself and looked back again at Mrs. Hudson. I was quite nonplussed by all of this this, and I asked her to explain;

"So then, you are expecting more guests to this party of yours?" I queried. . .

"No room! No room!" - was the rejoinder to my question that I heard, but not from Mrs. Hudson - this was coming, incredibly, from Holmes, who had stolen away while I was distracted and had now returned and was seated at one end of the table in an even more outlandish outfit - this time garishly dressed as a shop man of some sort, with an enormously large and ill-fitting top hat and, rather crudely, with the price slip still attached - 10/6.

Not knowing quite what to do, I followed Mrs. Hudson's nod and walked over to the opposite end of the table facing Holmes and started to seat myself.

"Not there!" he shouted "It's already taken! And even if it wasn't, it would surely be reserved for the King of Scandinavia, who, on very good authority as I have it, has been seen recently in this neighbourhood no later than one hour hence."

Yes, indeed; so I followed *his* nod and sat down two chairs from his right, and began to stare mouth agape at this most *outré* sight.

And then he said; "Now then Doctor, you *do* realise that you are late do you not? And it is not good enough for you to claim that the hansom lost a wheel on the way over because, by Jove, it had another perfectly good one, and therefore you should have arrived here in exactly no less than twice the time that it would have taken you otherwise, rather!"

As I watched him closely, I couldn't believe what was coming from his lips, and it seemed rather like a dream, and I pinched my thigh to make sure that I was indeed awake and not really experiencing a nightmare.

And then Mrs Hudson said, "Now then Dr.Watson, you will certainly be having two lumps, or four lumps, or no lumps at all, just as you please, very well then!"

"Phoo, Mrs Hudson", said Holmes," you can well imagine, my good woman, that this person sitting here may not be any sort of doctor at all and may very well be an imposter - Observe: You see that watch chain coming out of the lower side lateral-seamed vest pocket at an angle of approximately 17.42 degrees, do you? Well then, according to my extensive researches and inquires at the Royal Naval Observatory, this type of chain - and *only* this type - is well known and indeed is verifiable beyond a doubt to be occasionally worn only by certain tribes of Chinese tiger trainers who frequent but do not necessarily live in the frosted lower steppe regions of Upper Mongolia during the summer months and are given to playing a rather rude form of what the Americans call 'checkers', but what is not any sort of officially recognized kind of British activity at all , no-how, and therefore, how dare you - "Doctor" - to be trying to deliberately mislead my landlady into thinking that you are of such a kind and stature that you will not have to be paying for your tea."

"Your reasons for this, please -

"Come then - *roundly, roundly. . .*"

"Yes, your reasons - "Doctor" - HA!" Mrs. Hudson added, throwing her head back pertly as she spoke.

I was scarcely able to draw breath, and indeed had begun to feel faint as I sat in on this insanity, but I felt somehow compelled to answer - this *was* still Sherlock Holmes, after all - and so I thought for a moment, and composed myself as best I could, and said; "Holmes, you do remember the affair that I wrote-up but never quite finished that concerned the tradesman who was shanghaied and then was take. . ."

"Rubbish! Why, what has that got to do with anything? And why haven't you finished your biscuit yet? You well know that we must hurry and feed the alligators or the rates will go up as surely as there is a kilt in Scotland!"

Seeing that a direct approach was not succeeding, I decided to try to match him on his own grounds - but this being Holmes. . .

"Well then, since you won't answer my other question, why do you think you can get away with wearing *that* to a funeral for a magistrate? Don't you know that you can be arrested for wearing a maroon sweater with a chocolate-coloured vest and an orange necktie?"

"HA! There! Caught you!" he barked, "There is not even any such a thing as a chocolate-covered orange magistrate's marooned necktie!

"My dear fellow, if you insist on making any further such outbursts, I am afraid that we shall have to withdraw your desert option and, regrettably, take you up on your incessant offer for the cleaning-up of the parlour *and* the hallway instead of your usual living-room-only charge."

"Now, will that be in coal or in pounds sterling?

"And do make up your mind quickly, for as you well know, I have a concert tonight at the Palladium to play the eighteen *études* of Paganini and I only have enough change left in my pocket for the first twelve - so then - old chap - Lend me a fiver will you Watson, dear fellow?"

I was suddenly astonished; in his eyes was the old gleam and the smile rolled broadly up his face and cheeks as I had seen it a thousand times before when he addressed me in that particular manner.

"'Trick or Treat' I believe is the phrase, is it not, Mrs. Hudson?"

"Indeed it is, Mr. Holmes. And a right fine trick we played on the right honourable Doctor John H. Watson!"

Art Thou Privy~Mike B

"Art thou privy to a party, of a one called Moriarty,
One whose crimes all rise above those of the robber and the boor?
Dost thou know that reputation is the envy of the nation
Of the criminals and villains that *he* halted by the score?
And the reason for my rapture? *I alone* escaped his capture -
All the rest are resting buried or on rotting prison floors.
And by scheming and by cheating I've arranged a final meeting
'Twixt the two of us, although now only I know of its shore -
Near the misty falls of Reichenbach, both of us will walk a walk
From which, but only one returns - the other, *nevermore. . ."*

The Grave Dilemma~Jennnifer Emerson

Reprinted by special permission of Dr John H Watson, Late of the Army Medical Department, 1922.

FOREWORD:

Throughout the years of my long association with Sherlock Holmes, there have been many times when we have found ourselves in less than usual circumstances. Our efforts on behalf of those who sought our help did on occasion produce the most peculiar outcomes. Sometimes we helped people in ways we could never have imagined. One of those cases has haunted me to this day. It was an adventure which, for reasons that are entirely my own, I have not even dared lift my pen to record.

Until today.

It falls to me now to tell for the first time what really happened on that fateful night, twenty five years ago.

In this particular adventure, Holmes and I had ended up in a God-forsaken country cemetery. Held up behind a low and crumbling stone wall, we were eluding the barrage of gunfire from our opponents, who until a moment ago had numbered three.

 "Good shot, Watson!" said Holmes, "Who would have

thought that a simple case of jewel robbery could have proven to be so stimulating?"

"Yes, fascinating," said I as ducked back down. I heard another bullet bounce off the wall. Getting stuck in a damp, mouldy graveyard. Wonderful. Just where I envisioned myself on a Saturday evening in autumn; pursuing thieves for some purpose as yet unknown to me. We only just arrived in Canterbury this afternoon and briefly met our client, Miss Emily Middleston. The maid had prepared a good hot meal, and you drag me out of that nice warm Manor without even an explanation. Why do you never tell me anything, Holmes?"

"Watson, please. You whine worse than Mrs Hudson. And what have I told you about that pawky humour?"

"Oh, stuff it, old man. Keep still and let me take a look at that arm."

"Scratches, dear fellow. Nothing to signify."

"Nonsense. In this place even a slight flesh wound is prone to infection."

The bullet hadn't gone very deep in truth. Having nothing else (my bag was back at Middleston Manor – where my supper also lingered), I wrapped Holmes's black muffler around his left forearm and made a sling. He winced slightly as I tightened the knot. "That will have to do until we get back to the Manor."

Holmes gave me one of his patented second-long grins, "Thank you, Watson. And speaking of Middleston Manor, shall we make our exit?"

I glared at him, "Holmes, have you ever dodged bullet fire? Suffice to say it isn't exactly a picnic."

"Nonsense. There are now only two of those thugs remaining and we're both armed and able to return fire. And if you will look up, you will observe that the clouds are now moving more swiftly than before, covering the moon for longer intervals. I judged that last covering to be at least one minute and fifteen seconds long. That is more than enough time to escape a whole menagerie of ruffians. If you show yourself exactly thirty seconds before the next cloud covering –"

"Show myself? Holmes, you told me that you hadn't

injected —"

He rolled his eyes and held up his right hand in protest, "I only mean that they must see a trace of you, my dear Watson. Hold up your bowler or something. By my calculations they are nearly out of ammunition, so they will have no chance to shoot at us while we run, as they will be reloading. Unless of course, your leg, dear fellow -"

I fully cocked the hammer of my revolver, "To hell with my leg, Holmes. Let's go."

"Tsk, tsk, Watson. Such language. Clearly you must have been in the army."

"Now who's using pawky humour? Right, ready." I held up my bowler on a stick, just above the edge of the wall, and watched it sail into the air from the bullets that struck it. When the clouds covered the moon again, I stood up and made a run for it, making good headway. It happened just as Holmes had predicted, and soon I could hear him following after me. But the darkness didn't lift this time, and Holmes and I were consequently separated. I could just make out a faint outline of a stone crypt about twenty feet ahead, and made for it with all speed. When I got there, I leaned against the ancient door and caught my breath.

"Holmes? Holmes?" I whispered as loudly as I dared.

But he gave no reply. Just then I heard a bullet ricochet off a nearby tree. It was at that moment that I felt a powerful, burning scratch on my forehead. The force of the blow hurled me back and sent me stumbling through the decrepit door into the crypt. I landed hard against a raised sarcophagus. I scrambled around it and groped with my hands to find a wall. When I found it, the brick crumbled and gave way. The last thing I remember was falling.

When I came to, I was lying in a pile of rubble. Other than a slightly sore head from that bullet graze, I was unharmed. My revolver had fallen out of my hand as I fell, but I easily recovered it after a brief search of the immediate area. Through the darkness, faint glints of light were visible some distance away. Hushed voices were also coming from that direction. I crept closer as quietly as I could.

"Mercy, what a struggle," said one voice, "He were a clever one."

"Aye, but not clever enough by half," said the other. "And now there's no one to stop us from searching. Soon the jewels will be ours."

Oh my God…Holmes…No…Please no…

The first voice I had heard laughed menacingly, "No, not ours, Thomas. Mine."

I heard a gunshot and then the sounds of a struggle. At that point I could see two thieves fighting. But they were not the ones that Holmes and I had been pursuing. They had only two small crude tin lanterns. From the brightness (or more to the point the lack thereof), I could tell that the lanterns were lit by candles, not kerosene.

An open sarcophagus was nearby, the lid turned to reveal its contents. The newly dead corpse of a man was half extricated from it, lying face up over the edge. He looked to have been dead for about a month. His back was contorted in an unnatural angle. And thankfully Holmes was nowhere in sight. But it was the oddity of the clothes on the body that struck me. They were not modern at all, but in the style of a century ago. I wondered whether that blow to my head had been more serious than I had first thought. But even from that distance, as the two thieves rifled around on the floor, I could see that they were also dressed in an antiquated fashion – breeches, stockings, buckled shoes, hair tied back with ribbons, and long waistcoats covering their shirts.

Beyond where they were feuding was another stone tomb. I watched as a young girl peered from around one side of it in horror, just in time to see Thomas stabbed by the other thief. He fell lifeless to the ground. Terrified, she turned to run but tripped over one of the tools strewn and on the floor. The thief rushed her and dragged her up onto the top of the half open sarcophagus. I didn't yet have a clear shot at him, and I moved closer with all the stealth I could muster.

"Insufferable little wench!" said the brute, "I killed your brother easily enough. For your insolence you shall die alone in darkness with only your father's withering flesh for solace." He pointed with his blood-soaked knife into the tomb to indicate her intended location. Then he traced her bodice with his knife, "But first, tell me where those pretty baubles are, my darling Grace, or I'll –"

She shrieked and he struck her just as I reached the edge of the room. I raised my revolver and fired. But he seemed unharmed by the bullet, and rounded on me. I fired again, and to my horror heard only a hollow click. He swung and I ducked, striking the butt of my pistol into his kneecap. Another crack on the head brought him down. I ran over to the girl, who had fallen off of the lid and onto the floor.

"It's alright, now Miss. I'm a doctor. Please, let me help you."

She was a small girl and looked to be about fifteen if she was a day; a very comely girl with dark hair, dark eyes and porcelain skin. I pressed my handkerchief to her cheek and began to examine her ankle.

"Leave me be!" she ordered, and wriggled to get away.

"Miss, I give you my word that I am not with them. I fell down here from upstairs."

"Keep away, I say!"

"Stop fidgeting or you could worsen your injuries," She was looking in the direction of Thomas's body with inconsolable grief. "I'm sorry about your brother, Miss. Who is the other?"

"The other is William Stone, his friend and partner. But explain your presence, sir! What is your business here if, as you say, you are no thief? I do not know you."

The girl clearly had spirit, a quality which I admire in a female, and I smiled at her. "Doctor John Watson at your service, Miss. Now please show me the way out of here and I'll tell you anything you like. Perhaps you shouldn't walk on that ankle. If I carry you will you carry one of those lanterns?"

But the look on her face told me she didn't completely trust me and she began to cry very softly, "I'm afraid."

"My dear child, if it were my intention to harm you, wouldn't I have done it by now?"

The girl pondered this for a moment, and then looked at me. "Aye, I suppose that is true." She took the lantern from me and allowed me to lift her up. I cradled her as gently as if she were a baby. The girl was very cold to the touch, but yet did not shiver. Though it could easily be dismissed as a symptom of shock, it reminded me strangely of another type of cold which I had felt many times before. I knew it was best to keep her talking and conscious.

"May I have the pleasure of your name, Miss?"

"Miss Grace Middleston."

"Middleston!" I exclaimed.

"Aye."

"Delighted, Miss Middleston, though I don't see how I could have missed you. I thought I had met all of the family already. Still, I am happy to make your acquaintance, albeit under such wretched circumstances." She said nothing in return, and though she was still sniffling, I felt her form relax a bit in my arms.

At long last we emerged up a set of stone steps that looked in good condition. As we reached the top, I saw that the steps led up to a solid wall. Miss Middleston bade me pause while she touched a brick on the wall. It revealed an opening which led directly back into the top chamber. As soon as we had crossed the threshold, the wall closed behind us.

Torches were now lit in the main chamber, revealing it was clean and well kept. I recognized the door which I had stumbled through earlier, but it was shiny and still barred from the inside! To give my shoulder a rest, I set my young and lovely charge down on top of one of the raised tombs and wrapped my coat around her shoulders.

"I don't understand, Miss Middleston. This cannot be the

way I came in."

"This is the only way in, Doctor."

"It cannot be. The door I fell against was rusted and decayed. I fell through it as if it were a paper window, as I did through the back wall down into that burial chamber."

"I say again, good sir, this is the only way in from the outside. As you have seen that wall through which we just came contains a secret panel leading up from the chamber below in which my parents lie – and - now - Thomas…" She was doing her best not to cry again, and it made my heart break for her. This child was far too young to be on her own. Then her expression sharpened, "But it cannot be opened from this side. The opening mechanism is in another part of this room. William must have found out."

"What is his connection to you, Miss?"

"He was my fiancé. Aye, I was promised to him when I was little. In truth I did not like him. He was a bad influence over my brother, and cared only for wealth. Father was the heir to a rare collection of jewels. Thomas was to inherit them upon Father's death, and they would fall to me if Thomas died because my little sister Emily is not yet six. But Thomas had quarreled with Father and left for London with William. Father disowned him, released me from my engagement with William, and ordered that the jewels be hidden. The stonemasons were given instructions to create a special place in the chamber down below in which to hide them. Only I know where they are. I was coming here tonight to visit my parents. Then I heard sounds and hid. It was William and Thomas. I – I couldn't get out -"

"Miss Middleston, calm yourself. Where is that panel?"

"I shall not tell you that easily. Besides, you are bleeding, Good Sir." She withdrew her own handkerchief and dabbed at my forehead. The soft linen smelled of orange flower water. Her icy touch was feather light, and she sighed. "You are so warm. I haven't felt such warmth in so long. Perhaps I can trust you."

"I assure you that you can, Miss Middleston. Mr. Holmes and I are here pursuing thieves who wish to steal those jewels that you nearly gave your life for."

"Mr. Holmes?"

"Yes, my friend, Mr. Sherlock Holmes," I said proudly.

"I do not know that name."

"Surely you have read of our cases in *The Strand Magazine*?"

"What be this – ma-gaz-ine?"

Now I feared that the poor girl was suffering from a tremendous case of shock. It was then for the first time that I realized she too was dressed in 18th century clothing as Thomas and William had been. It was a most becoming gown of green silk with a matching ribbon tied around her neck, which was also adorned by a cascade of curls down one side. "Ah ha! Now I see. You are dressed this way because it is All Hallow's Eve! No doubt those two were dressed that way to avoid capture. Why, anyone would think they were real ghosts!"

She pressed her small hand lightly over my lips, "Hush, Doctor, I beseech you. Speak not of such things here."

I took her hand and held it reassuringly, "Oh my dear, don't you see? That combined with the shock has confused you a bit. Of course! How absurdly simple. Why didn't I think of it before?"

She lowered her gaze from mine, "There are things that you, Doctor, even with all your knowledge and skill, do not understand."

I smiled and tilted her chin back up, "Then why don't you explain it to me?"

But she remained adamant, "God sir, do you not know that on this night the dead may assume corporeal form, and can roam at will? Take care, Doctor Watson. On this night not all is as it seems. And I – No, I shall say no more of it; for I have told you too much already."

At that I chuckled, "Well, don't you worry about a thing. You are in the company of one of Her Majesty's soldiers. I am a retired Army surgeon."

She giggled, "Forgive me sir, but surely you mean His Majesty? Perhaps you had better rest too, lest that small wound on your head does you any further ill."

"His Majesty? My dear girl, Queen Victoria is on the throne."

She frowned at me, "Nay, it is His Majesty King George III." That confirmed it. As I had thought, a severe case of shock.

"Oh never mind." I stood up to reach down into my coat pocket, "I'll reload my revolver and we'll be –" But there were no bullets left. "That's odd, I know I had another full round at least in here. The bullets must have fallen out when I fell down that hole." I tucked the revolver back into the empty pocket, "Speaking of which, from what you said earlier, these two raised tombs are false, are they not?"

"Aye, this one (referring to the she was now sitting on) slides to reveal another staircase, but only if it is manipulated correctly. Father allowed me to help him design it."

"So there is one entrance and one exit from that chamber below and each of those passages, each only accessible from their respective directions? Clever girl."

She frowned, "Nay, not clever enough. William discovered the entrance."

I bent back down to her and patted her hand. "Miss Middleston, don't blame yourself. Greed knows no bounds. The likes of him are unworthy of a young lady like you."

In the candlelight I could see that she had blushed ever so slightly. "I thank you, good Sir." And then she kissed my cheek.

Now it was my turn to blush. "Well, I say, that just made the whole blasted evening worthwhile! Shall we get you home?"

"Home!" She threw her arms around my neck and laughed with delight, "Oh how I have longed to go home! Please, let us not tarry here a moment longer and go there now! I miss my sister Emily so much. No, you needn't carry me, I think I can walk. My ankle feels much better."

"Very well, maybe it's only a slight sprain. It's hard to tell with only one candle to see with. Now up you come, my dear, let's get —"

I was interrupted by a harsh and familiar voice.

"Harlot! You would not have me, but you flaunt your virtue at a stranger? A common soldier?" The secret wall panel was open again and there stood William Stone, blood trailing down from where I had struck him. "Did you think it would be that easy to be rid of me, Grace? You shall never leave me or this crypt!"

"No, William!" Miss Middleston cried. Stone began to stagger toward us, the same bloody knife still in his hand. I helped Miss Middleston down and we ran to the door. I lifted the bar and opened it.

"Run, Miss Middleston! Do not wait for me!"

She wasted no time and dashed out the door. I shut and barred it again just in time to see William two feet away from me. He brandished his knife high over his head and closed the distance between us. It was in that same moment that my forehead began to ache and the room began to spin worse than if I had consumed a whole bottle of brandy. Then all went dark.

"Watson! Watson! Wake up, old fellow!"

My head was throbbing. As my eyes opened I beheld the image of Sherlock Holmes hovering close above me.

"Holmes?"

"Yes, my dear Watson. Thank heaven we found you. Here, sit up slowly now. Constable, help me sit him up. Easy Watson, take it slow. You've sustained two lacerations on the head. The one on the front appears to be a graze from a bullet. The other is a rather nasty crack on the back of your head no doubt caused by the impact of falling down in here."

Once I was in a seated position, I could make out where I was. I was in the same rubble pile I had found myself in when I had fallen through the floor earlier! And I was wearing my coat!

"How did I get back down here? That fellow must have thrown me back down."

"Who?" asked the Constable.

"William Stone. Have you seen him? Oh God – where is Miss Middleston?" I grabbed Holmes's coat. "Did you find her?

Surely you must have seen her running out of the crypt."

"You mean Miss Emily Middleston?" said Holmes, "My dear Watson, our client is still at the Manor waiting for us. Calm down."

"No, no, Miss Grace Middleston! Where is she? I saw her! Stone killed her brother and then attacked her. The savage brute; what he would've done to her if I hadn't been there! We must find her, Holmes! He'll kill her!" By now the exertion of the past few seconds had sent blood rushing into and consequently out of my head. I fell back against Holmes's shoulder.

Holmes tightened his grip, "Watson, calm yourself. There is no one else here. My dear fellow, you have suffered trauma to the head. You must have been hallucinating. We'll get you back to the Manor now. Those two thieves we eluded earlier tonight were easy enough to catch and are now in the hands of the local police."

They helped me up. In the light of the police lanterns, I could see the burial chamber ahead. It was untouched. Old and dusty, but untouched. There was no sign of any grave desecration, Thomas's body, William, or Grace. The staircase which led to the surface was where it had been. But that, like the chamber above, was no longer new. Rather, they were moldy, neglected, and laden with ancient cobwebs. I was too stunned to speak. I knew Holmes was worried enough about me and decided to hold my tongue rather than upset him more.

Once back at the Manor, Holmes and I were helped upstairs and tended to. I protested the sleeping powder that the local doctor offered me. But the look of worry on Holmes's face won out and I took the glass.

A while later I woke to find Miss Emily Middleston watching over me. I wasted no time in asking her a few pointed questions about Grace. The look of shock on her face was one I will remember until the day I leave this earth.

"My God, Doctor," she whispered, her hand reaching instinctively to her throat, "You saw her. I never have, but Grandmother used to talk about Grace all the time."

"Please, Miss Middleston, tell me everything you know."

"Miss Grace Emily Middleston was my Great-Grand Aunt. Her little sister, Emily Patience Middleston, was my grandmother for whom I am named. Poor Grace died young and no one knows exactly what happened. A grave has never been found."

I shuddered; I knew where it was. "Did she – did she just vanish, then?"

"Why yes, Doctor Watson, she did. The legend states that she went to the family crypt to pay her respects to her parents one night, and was never seen again. Grandmother said she was lovely and had raven-colored hair and dark eyes. Her favorite color was green, and her scent was orange flower water. She loved stories of brave knights and soldiers. A true little romantic, I dare say."

Now I swallowed hard. "Miss Middleston, is the date of Grace's disappearance recorded?"

"Yes. In fact it was one hundred years ago tonight, the thirty-first of October, 1797. Oh dear, Doctor, are you alright? You've grown even paler. Shall I call back the doctor?"

"No! Please continue. Please."

"Very well if you'll settle back down. That's better. Legend has it that Grace's spirit is trapped in the tomb until a man of lion-hearted courage frees her. You see, she cannot leave the crypt of her own accord, and waits for someone brave enough to help her. But no one has dared to venture in there since the search was abandoned all those decades ago. After her mysterious disappearance, none of the other family members would be buried there, and the crypt fell into disrepair. That is all I know, Doctor Watson. No one believed in the jewels anymore, either, until those thieves decided to plan an investigation of their own tonight. Thank God you and Mr Holmes arrived in time to help our police stop them."

"And what of Grace's brother, Thomas? What of William Stone?"

"Their fates are mentioned nowhere in the family records."

I closed my eyes and fought back a choking sensation in my throat, "Poor Grace. But, Miss Middleston, the legend says that she cannot leave the crypt of her own power. Tonight, I let her out of the crypt. I opened the door for Grace and she ran through it!"

She grabbed my hand, "Doctor Watson, do you think that Grace is free at long last? Oh I hope so. Tell me something, was she as pretty as Grandmother Emily said?"

"My dear young lady, she was a radiant beauty."

"God bless you, Doctor. Now please rest."

I obeyed. "Thank you, Miss Middleston.

She patted my hand, "Emily."

"Thank you, Miss Emily."

She left the room briefly only to come back with a pot of tea and some biscuits. It smelled wonderful, and my stomach reminded me that it was still empty, so I asked her put extra cream and sugar in my cup. Beside the biscuit plate, I noticed something else on the tea tray.

"What is that?"

"Oh, it's for you. My servant complained to me that she could hear footsteps earlier coming from the study. I have my writing desk and legal papers in there and so keep the room locked when I am away. But I have not left the house today, so the room was open. At any rate, she refused to go in, and so I did. The room was untouched, but I discovered this little parcel on the table. It is addressed to you, Doctor, and I thought perhaps it was from London. No doubt the maid put it in there when it arrived and is adding the story about the footsteps to give her Mistress a little Halloween scare."

"That's impossible. No one in London knows where I am, not even Mrs Hudson."

She set the teapot back down on the tray with just a hint of a tremor. "Well," she said nervously, "be that as it may, it's for

116

you. I'll just go and look in on Mr Holmes. I'll be back soon." And thus she left me staring at the small and curious parcel, delicately tied in a green silk ribbon. A small bit of parchment was tucked under the ribbon on which was written in fine script, 'To Dr John H Watson, My Gallant Gentleman & Soldier'. With trembling hands I picked it up, undid the bow, and held my breath. It was a carefully folded but bloodstained handkerchief that bore the monogram, 'G. E. M.' The blood on that handkerchief was mine! Grace had used it to dab my forehead. Nearly overcome, I lifted the dainty cloth to my nose and detected the delicious aroma of orange flower water.

Underneath that handkerchief was another, also bloodstained with the monogram of 'J. H. W.' staring up at me. It was my handkerchief, the very same one I had used on her cold, fair cheek. Now my handkerchief was carefully wrapped around something. Upon peering inside, I saw my six missing bullets. I hurled myself out of bed and flew to the nearby window. As I threw it open, the clock struck midnight. Below, though some distance from the front door, I could see a small figure turn into the foggy night, and caught a glint of green satin shimmering in the moonlight.

A knock on the door nearly made me hit the ceiling.

"Watson? Are you alright? Miss Middleston said you were up."

Holmes and Miss Emily came through the door in the next instant. I tucked my treasure into my dressing gown pocket before they could see.

"What the devil are you doing up, dear fellow? From the noise I thought you fell out of bed. Get back under the covers and drink your tea, Doctor. That is an order."

I was still too shocked from my revelation to argue and allowed Holmes to assist me.

"Holmes, your arm-"

"Will be fine, Watson. I told you it was merely a scratch. Now, lie still. Here, drink this tea."

My hands were shaking so badly that Holmes had to hold the saucer while I took a few sips.

"Watson, what is the matter?" asked Holmes as he turned away from us to set down my tea up on the nightstand. Miss Emily saw that the parcel was no longer on the tea tray, and I put my finger to my mouth to stop her from asking.

"Nothing Holmes. Just Halloween jitters, I suppose."

"Oh now really, Watson," said Holmes as he turned back to face us, "That is a ridiculous assertion, even for someone who reads yellow-backed novels," he said as he winked at me.

I smiled back, "They're not all I read, you know."

He raised a caustic eyebrow, "Indeed?"

"Indeed." I looked over at Miss Emily and took a deep breath,

> " 'And thou art dead, as young and fair
>
> As aught of mortal birth;
>
> And form so soft, and charms so rare,
>
> Too soon returned to Earth!
>
> Though Earth receiv'd them in her bed,
>
> And o'er the spot the crowd may tread.
>
> In carelessness or mirth,
>
> There is an eye which could not brook,
>
> A moment on that grave to look.' "*

Miss Middleston put her hand to her mouth, "Oh Doctor Watson. That was beautiful."

"Thank you. I only wish I could take the credit for writing it. It describes a certain…someone…very well, don't you think?"

She smiled at me, "Yes, Doctor Watson. It does indeed."

Holmes looked over at her and then at me, "Um, yes. A quaint little rhyme, Watson, to be sure. Shelley?"

"No."

He thought for a moment, "Ah Ha! Poe?"

"No," I said, and took another sip of tea, "Byron."

Miss Middleston stifled a giggle.

"Blast," muttered Holmes, "Oh well, the florid and romantic is your department, dear Watson. Miss Middleston, if you will kindly pass me that plate. Here, care for a biscuit, old man?"

EPILOGUE:

With our business successfully concluded, Holmes and I left for London a week later. Before we left I did show Miss Emily my secret parcel. I offered Grace's handkerchief to her, since it could be considered a family heirloom. But she insisted that I should keep it as Grace had intended. We both concluded that the parcel was Grace's confirmation that she had indeed been saved from a fate worse than death, and we have heard no more from her since. Not a day goes by that I do not think of My Little Lady From Long Ago, and though I have never shown it to anyone (not even to Holmes), I keep those two handkerchiefs and the bullets tucked away in an unobtrusive place of honour in my room.

To this very day, the Middleston jewels have never been found, and wild horses couldn't drag their location out of me. There they lie still, safely where Grace put them in the secret burial chamber so long ago. And that is as it should be. But I like to think that the real treasure is mine - forever locked safely in a deep and sacred corner of my heart.

Snow~Jane Stuart

I button up my collar and I flex my stiffened shoulder and I strive
to see my partner in the feeble light remaining.
A busy day in clinic calls for slippers by the fire not a midnight
jaunt through London; though I'm really not complaining.

~o~

It's raining.

~o~

I'd been home, perhaps five minutes, and was ready for my
supper when my partner bustled in, and barked a hurried, harried
greeting.
He requested my assistance in surveillance of a building. He
suspected an alliance; an unholy villains' meeting.

~o~

Now it's sleeting.

~o~

So, abandoning hot supper and discarding cosy slippers, I took up
my old revolver (and a sandwich from the larder).
As we headed out together, I was told in sketchy detail, of a
stolen hoard of silver and a missing Scotland Yarder.

~o~

Sleeting harder.

~o~

I followed Holmes in silence; slipping softly through the shadows, though I really had no clue precisely who my friend was trailing.
I could sense his concentration as he tracked our quarry's movements; for the missing Scotland Yarder was the price he'd pay for failing.

~o~

It's hailing.

~o~

Now, I'm crouched behind some bushes while my partner checks the building; he's been gone for six long minutes and my apprehension's growing.
Do I wait until the signal, as my comrade has instructed? Or has Holmes encountered trouble? There's no easy way of knowing.

~o~

Now it's snowing.

~o~

One more minute, then I'll follow, if his signal fails to reach me.
As I count each passing second, the suspense is agonizing.

A distant gunshot echoes through the whirling, swirling snowflakes; and I'm up and out and running. Fear for Holmes is galvanizing.

~o~

Storm is rising.

~o~

I hurtle through the entrance with revolver at the ready, I'm quite heedless of the danger; it's my comrade's fate which matters.

Holmes stands helplessly at gunpoint, as his captor pulls the trigger. And I bless my army training; roll and fire; his weapon shatters.

~o~

Blizzard batters.

~o~

Holmes ducks down, then dives to tackle the remaining, startled villain. I stand up and rub my shoulder (I'd forgotten it was aching.)
We release the bound inspector, and survey the missing silver. Soon the place is filled with Yarders; a successful undertaking.

~o~

Storm is breaking.

~o~

Danger over; Holmes regards me with a dry, amused expression;
"Your grand entrance, my dear Watson, though quite late, was not
displeasing."
I glare back, "Don't fault my timing! Next time act with greater
caution!" But he knows I've got the message underneath his
gentle teasing.

~o~

Storm is easing.

~o~

Task complete, we wander homeward through the sleeping streets
of London. Snow is falling now, more gently; light as silk or
swans down feather.
Breakfast, tea, a change of clothing and a blazing fire are waiting.
One more case, in which we've proved that we're unbeatable,
together.

~o~

Perfect weather.

A Halloween Visit~David Ruffle

"She will not return, Watson. Forgive my bluntness."

I had been pacing the room for some time now and Holmes could not have failed to notice my agitation. It had been a few short months since my dear wife had departed this life and with it being the evening of October 31st when boundaries between the spirit world and the living become somewhat blurred I was hopeful of a sign of any kind that Mary was at peace. Was I expecting a visitation? I cannot in all conscience say yes, but how sweet it would be to gaze on her likeness once more.

"Your analytical reasoning may lead you to such a conclusion Holmes, but I am a creature of emotion and passion."

"And if you were to see a phantom of your late wife, how could you be sure it was not a phantasm of the brain projected onto your surroundings by your grief and your need?"

"Perhaps I would not be sure. Either way, Holmes I would be comforted beyond measure and my grief assuaged."

"To be blunt with you Watson, the dead do not walk the earth. Their shades do not return either to comfort or assuage."

"I need to believe and your coldness at a time like this does you no credit at all if I may speak bluntly too."

"Oh friend Watson. My abject apologies if you perceive me as cold. I care about you my dear fellow and what this folly may do to you. Halloween and its origins are now so shrouded in mystery that we cannot be sure that it had anything to do with spirits and the like. And besides if ghosts truly existed why would they have need to wait until an arbitrarily appointed day on the calendar to appear?"

"There is an element of truth in what you say Holmes, but spirits and revenants have appeared in their multitudes over the years. Can all the eye-witnesses to these supernatural sights and sounds have been mistaken? I believe firmly that we have a soul and this soul survives in some fashion and can reveal itself to us, perhaps only in time of great need."

"The soul returns then in the guise of its former body then is the gist of what you say, Watson?"

"Yes."

"Do clothes have souls then? Why do not these spirits return to us naked?"

"It may be a question of propriety Holmes."

"Oh, Watson it will not do, it really won't."

"Then how do you account for the tales of ghost spanning thousands of years be it Halloween or any other time?"

"I have to admit that I have not given it a great deal of thought over the years and I have no data to enable me to come to conclusions in individual cases, but I do have a theory of my own Watson. Namely, that ghosts are not, as I have expressed, the dead coming back to walk among us, but rather they are living, breathing human beings."

"Preposterous, Holmes. How could that be?"

"Bear with me. If we look at time as a continuous loop then we can surely perceive of times when that loop become misshapen and folds in on itself. I believe the result of this is a time anomaly whereby a window of sorts opens up and enables some people to see what is happening in a bygone time for a short while."

"It seems to me to be outlandish in the extreme, but we will have to agree to differ on this occasion Holmes For me ghosts are indeed the spirits of the dead and this is something I will always believe."

"My final words on the subject, painful as they might be to you on this All Hallows Eve is that there are no such things as ghosts. I would stake the whole of any reputation I may have garnered over the years on that statement."

We resumed our silence. My heart was still full of longing

and I knew rest would not come easily to me. The silence seemed to grow even more marked and I was aware that my name was being called, faintly as though whispered in the wind. The gas lights dimmed and flickered creating dancing shadows on the walls for an instant. Then I was aware of another shadow which appeared to me to step out of the very fabric of the wall itself. This shadow grew more substantial by the second, changing rapidly until my own sweet Mary stood before me. Radiant and beautiful as in life.

"I have little time John. I wish you peace and please take very good care of yourself. I love you now as I did then."

I have no clear recollection of my response to these words. I told her I loved her and always would, I know that much. Within a few seconds she had faded once more into the shadows and melted into the wall from whence she had came. I was overcome for more than a few minutes and had given little thought to Holmes while this extraordinary event was unfolding. However as I glanced at him now, I saw a man in shock, his mouth open, his eyes staring at that point on the wall where the image of my wife had returned. I poured my friend a large brandy and brought it to his lips. I brought my mouth to his ear.

"Norbury," I whispered.

Eyes of Grey~Grace Smoczyk

Eyes of grey…

Like a rainy day

They sparkle with a mischievous glint

Like a dime – fresh from the mint

They perceive the darkest secrets of an ordinary stranger

They narrow and darken in times of danger

These fateful eyes pierce the veil of time-

They observe the clues of an evil crime

Growing hard at villains does not well bode-

Squinting deep in thought at a complex code

Or staring vacantly into space

As the mind races to solve a case

They go wide and bright from a certain solution,

The brain not caring that the drug's a pollution

Dancing with delight – like an actors' on stage

Flashing and sparking in anger or rage

They grow dim with fear

Or soften….when a friend is near

Heavy, deep, and burdened are they, with many cares

Holding the deep dark secrets his soul bears

Beautiful…magnetic…troubling things are they….

Beloved Sherlock's….
….eyes of grey.

Rats and Cats~Mike Wichern

It was a dark day in November
When we sat down to remember
The chaos of Sherlock's ember
Running wild through old London town.

"What have you got there, Holmes?" I asked with genuine curiosity. My friend had taken some small phial out of his inner coat pocket and was attempting to warm it up by alternately rubbing it between his hands and shaking it. The look on his face was one of the utmost concern.

"I have here Watson, an ounce-worth of what I believed to be the luminescent compound used to such great effect on the hound of our last case. It has taken me some time to come up with the proper chemical proportions on my own. I think I have succeeded in that regard; however it seems I still need an outside catalyst to start the chemical reaction. I was hoping heat alone, or perhaps heat plus slight agitation, would do it, however that does not seem to be the case."

"I see." said I somewhat bemused and struggling to hold back a laugh. "Thinking of making your own demon hound, are you then?"

"Not quite, Watson."

"Mrs. Hudson has informed me that her cat has escaped the premises again. She sees the thing return every now and again, but is unable to catch it."

I interjected, "Holmes surely you don't mean to imply that you've taken to looking for lost pets to pass the time?"

"Indeed I have, Watson."

"But there are a million and one things you could be better using your time for than silly nonsense such as this. It's absurd!"

"I know Watson, but ever since I moved into this flat with you, it never fails that once she can get me aside, without you being around, Mrs. Hudson invariably asks me to go looking for one or another of her pets. I have consented in the past for want of keeping these furnishings at such a reasonable price and have, even when real cases have gotten the better of my time, taken to replacing her cat with another, similar looking, one. But I am afraid I can no longer do that as with her last pet, she has got herself a cat with six toes. Those are exceedingly rare to come by, especially in a colour matching hers." He looked at the phial once again, frowned, then proceeded over to the table and began looking through the jars of bulk chemicals he had kept there.

"But..." I said, "I don't exactly follow. What precisely are you planning to do with that concoction? You wouldn't dare poison a cat would you, Holmes?"

My friend noticing the slight urgency in my voice, paused for a moment as if to think something over, then said, "Don't be ridiculous Watson. You know I would do nothing of the sort. Can you really not see what I'm about to use this substance for?"

"No," said I, "I really can't possibly know."

A subtle, fleeting smile broke the corner of his mouth, but he continued looking over his store of chemicals without further delay and indeed without so much as an indication that he had heard my last statement save for the slight smile. It was at this time I felt the need to seek fresh air and to stretch my legs. Without another word spoken between us, I got up, grabbed my coat, and proceeded out into the unseasonably bracing October night air of London.

As I walked along the various streets and passed by the alleys which intercepted them in and around the buildings that surrounded our home, I couldn't help but notice the inordinate number of stray cats that seemed to be practically everywhere I looked. After some time I recalled from memory the last cat Mrs. Hudson had and made up my mind to keep an eye open for one resembling it. After some time however, I realised my efforts, just as my friend had pointed out earlier, were very much in vain and I gave it up and returned to Baker Street.

When I returned, I asked Mrs. Hudson if she had any news as to her cat, whereupon she answered, somewhat surprised, no she hadn't but she had faith in Holmes's abilities and that if anyone could find the cat, he could. I then entered our rooms and, seeing Holmes in the exact same place that I left him and knowing from past experience that he wouldn't be in a talkative mood, proceeded to go through without saying a word, and into my bedroom for a night's rest.

The next morning I awoke to find him once more at it just as he was before, only this time, and even with the morning sunlight coming into our windows, setting the whole flat alight in, what seemed to me, an unusual if not spectacularly bright yellow light, I saw in his hand the same phial filled with liquid, only I could clearly make out that it was itself emitting light!

"Holmes!" I said, "You've cracked it!"

"It would appear so." said he, "but this is only the first step."

"What do you mean?" said I confused, "Are you going to use this stuff to find Mrs. Hudson's missing cat?"

He looked back at me and apparently irritated with my last question he answered tersely, "Yes, that is precisely what I am going to do."

And with a slight pause, continued by answering the question I had in my mind but had yet to ask out loud, "You will find out soon enough. Now if you will excuse me I am off to see my old friend, the butcher." And with that he was off, leaving me once more to myself in our flat.

Over the next few days I hardly saw my friend at all. He was indeed on the case of Mrs. Hudson's missing cat, he assured me, but needed only a little time to bring it to completion. He told me to occupy my time as best I could and not to bother involving myself over such a case as this. I have to admit I thought his was a fool's errand and was delighted to not be asked to take part, but I couldn't help wonder from time to time as to how he was getting along. And of course I wanted to waste no time chronicling his success should he in fact be successful.

It was sometime the following week however, just before Halloween, when I caught up once again with Holmes. He looked quite the worse for wear. So pale and unusually thin, even for him, was he that he almost looked as if he'd either seen a ghost or was quickly on his way to becoming one.

"Holmes!" I exclaimed, "What have you been doing to yourself?"

With a slight smile he said, "Watson, would you believe me if I told you I am now the most wanted man in all of London? I have not slept in some three days. And I'm afraid our friend Lestrade thinks I've gone completely mad." He shook his head, then continued "No, Watson, this is not the place to discuss it. I have reserved us two rooms at a nearby acquaintance's house for the evening and possibly longer. I think we should go without further delay." And with that we were quickly into a cab and at our destination some short time later.

Once we were at the residence of Holmes' friends, they insisted upon seeing Holmes of having us both to dine with them. Holmes' initial reaction of not wanting them to be put out quickly changed to one of acquiescence and we sat down to one of the finest meals I have ever had the fortune to partake. The conversation that evening was one of local crime and criminals. The gentleman was, as it turned out, a barrister who was keenly aware of Holmes' abilities and successes in solving crimes the authorities always seemed to be outmatched by. The two reminisced quite a bit after dinner but it became immediately clear that as to the current case Holmes' was working on, no questions should be asked as none would be answered.

I waited for the opportunity to get Holmes aside with enough time to give him the chance to tell me what he meant when he made that most remarkable statement earlier about being the most wanted man in all of London, but to no avail. Our night quickly passed and before I knew it Holmes, looking quite a bit like a man rejuvenated, was shown his room and I to mine. I quickly fell asleep that night. It was unusual for me to do so, as I recall, for all the excitement I had had that day. It was however, not to be a full and restful night's sleep for me as sometime in the early hours of the following morning, October 31st to be precise, I was awakened, or so I thought by a slight otherworldly presence sitting atop my bed covers, just beyond my feet.

As I awoke and my eyes slowly began to focus, I saw two small rows of teeth complete with a tongue snaking in and out, hovering in the darkness, just inches over my feet. I was stunned into silence at seeing such a sight and could do no more than just simply hang onto the sheets, slowly inching them up to just beneath my nose, never for a second taking my eyes off those teeth.

After a few moments passed, the teeth began to bob and sway and I noticed that in their movements the tongue would lash out, peeling strips and bits of darkness off some seemingly grotesque body that was there, but otherwise invisible to me.

One strip was pulled. Then another. Then a pause. Then again. And again. Whatever the thing was, I wasn't sure, but what I was sure of was that it was materializing right there on my bed. And something worse was happening, for while I was looking at the one set of teeth and stripes, I could feel a presence of another invisible entity slowly walking across my bed towards the first. And another. And another. And they too all had sets of sharp glowing teeth and each, when settled, began tearing strips of darkness off their own bodies. Finally, in the darkness, when something made to craw underneath the covers with me, I made up my mind that what I was seeing was real and no dream.

I made to get out of bed, but stepped on something, something which let forth a haunting, low, and truly unholy cry. I stumbled. Then fell. And in getting back up, decided to make for the door, leaving the bed sheets, my sole protection behind. I stepped on something else. This time however, it was much smaller than the first thing. It couldn't have been much bigger than my own bare foot. But it let forth a terrible "screeee" and I stumble once again.

The other people in the house seemingly heard the last noise and I could hear them slowly getting out of bed, presumably to come to see what the racket was. At this time, and while still kneeling on the floor, I reached out in the darkness, hoping to find the knob to the door of my room to make an escape, all the while keenly becoming aware that the noise had aroused more than just my friends in the house but panic in the creatures within the room as well.

I could feel them, rather than hear or see them, running around behind me in the room and as I groped for the doorknob, I would catch fleeting glimpses of light from them moving around, which momentarily left behind glowing stripes in the pitch black room. They seemed to be fighting either themselves or some other invisible entity within the room, for the moment. And I was doubly determined to find the door before one side or the other won out and decided to turn their attention towards me.

Finally, half crawling, half stumbling, I found and turned the knob on a door that I subsequently noticed was already slightly ajar, pulled it to and stepped out into a hall which at this time was slowly becoming brighter as the lights from my fellow house members got closer and closer. I closed the door with a soft click, and fell back against the wall in the hall, half exhausted for my efforts.

Holmes was the first to find me in that state and looking once from me to the door then back again proceeded to ask me something, but then quickly reconsidered. He reached down and helped me up, taking me to his room where he laid me down upon his bed and told me to rest. He then left and that was the last I saw of him that night for I quickly fell back asleep not knowing if I was dreaming or not, but feeling very very tired. The next morning when I awoke in Holmes's room, I knew immediately that what had happened in the course of the night was not dream. I quickly decided to get dressed and upon doing so made my way back to my old room. On my way there however Holmes intercepted me and directed me to the kitchen where he said I was to have breakfast and have everything explained to me.

I was hardly two bites in to yet another great meal when I felt I could no longer hold back and I burst forth, somewhat more loudly than I had hoped it would be,

"What is going on in this house? And where the have have you been and what in the name of God have you been up too?" which, before anyone could answer, I followed with "You realise I could have been ki..."

Holmes interjected, looking somewhat embarrassed at our hosts, "DO not worry, Watson. Nothing of the sort would have happened to you here in this house."

Our hosts, much to my astonishment, both struggled to hold back from laughing at what I was about to say.

Holmes continued, "Watson, first off I must apologise for the way in which I have treated you of late. I have kept you far too much in the dark over matters which, I now see from another's perspective, as somewhat more than trivial or commonplace."

As he spoke I noticed two rather affectionate tabby cats enter into the room and make their way over to a saucer of milk placed on the floor just to the side of the sink. Then, to my surprise, a huge rat followed and joined in with the cats licking up the milk. Apart from the size and what it was doing, there was something else odd about the rat that I couldn't put my finger on. It seemed to know that I was looking at it and moved to the opposite side of the bowl so as to seemingly keep one of its beady eyes firmly upon me. The action sent chills up my spine. Upon catching my expression and understanding what I was thinking, Holmes offered forth an explanation.

"That rat is a tame rat, Watson. It along with four cats, two dogs, and a rabbit, is the pet of our hosts here, Mr and Mrs Brillstone."

I looked up and caught their smiling faces, saying simply, "Oh, well that explains why the cats don't eat it...I guess?"

"Quite so." said Holmes with a chuckle, "that and the fact that they are kept well fed, as you can see." He went on, "These animals, along with, (here he looked odd, as if slightly embarrassed about something) several other animals have been kindly offered by their owners for the chance to take part in a, rather unorthodox experiment. The very same experiment, whose beginnings you yourself were present and witness to back in

Baker Street."

"I don't understand." said I, "What do you mean by this?"

"Very well." said he, "I see that you're just about finished with breakfast, so I suppose it shouldn't wait any longer."

"Watson, you do remember when I made that discover about how precisely to concoct the luminescent compound?"

"Yes" I said, hoping he would continue.

"And you will no doubt recall that it was used to such great effect in one of our previous cases involving a hound?"

"Yes, I do. Please go on." I said.

"Well I got the idea to use that compound as a taggant..."

"A what?" said I.

"Forgive me" he said."A taggant normally, is a unique chemical compound put inside another chemical compound, one which it can in no way react to or with, for the purposes of being used to trace the compound. Law enforcement have used taggants for quite some time to trace potential bomb making materials, and companies working in the field of advanced chemistry sometimes employ the use of taggants to trace the suspected theft of proprietary materials they've developed. Do you follow me?"

"Yes," I said, "please go on."

"Well it occurred to me, after having the last lengthy conversation with Mrs Hudson," he paused, and then turned to our hosts asking, "You are familiar with our landlady?"

To which the answer came, "yes of course."

"Anyway," he began again, "Mrs Hudson had told me in that conversation that her cat in particular, could find its way through several fences, over a small outbuilding, and onto her back balcony every night to a saucer of milk that she put out for it. And although it would never appear when someone was present, she felt for certain it would come about when no one was around."

"Well, as you can imagine, this made things straightforward for me. I would simply wait and trap the creature at the earliest opportunity." He paused here, and then began again.

"That particular course of action was to come to naught,

as I am loath to admit, the cat was exceedingly wary and always seemed to sense my presence when I was around, or indeed any trap that I might set for it."

"So, as I said, I got the idea to use the luminescent compound we were introduced to in an earlier case as a chemical taggant. If I could only get the substance into the cat, I felt certain I could somehow track its comings and goings and eventually get the thing. So far I had a foolproof plan. If you will recall, I went around to the butchers, but what I didn't tell you was that I went there to pick up something to entice the cat to eat. I figured on putting the taggant into the meat, then wait for it to be eaten. Afterward it would only be a matter of time before someone spotted the cat and tell me, thus giving me a general idea of where the cat went when it wasn't at Mrs Hudson's house."

"Yes." I said, "I think I follow you. Seems like an interesting plan. Why didn't you want to let me help you?"

"Well, at first, it truly was because I thought it was such a simple case that you wouldn't want to bother with it. It held, as far as I could see, the potential for none of those moments of peculiarity, drama, or adventure that so often make up my rather better known cases. But that quickly changed."

"You see, contrary to Mrs Hudson's claim that only her cat could make its way to her balcony, I soon discovered nearly two dozen cats, five rats, and three pigeons, not to mention a whole host of insects, had made the trip as well. It was also soon apparent to me that, these creatures, when not at Mrs Hudson's balcony, were quickly becoming famous in their regular haunts. Alarmingly so. And for the past several weeks it has been my misfortune to have to accompany Lestrade, and a few of his more trustworthy fellow Scotland Yarders, on excursions in the city to the places where these animals go, to track them down and to, ehrm, reassure the surrounding residents that they have indeed not seem demon creatures on the prowl."

He looked at me, then at our hosts, and spoke once more, "Lestrade felt all the animals should be taken immediately outside of the city, to a farm somewhere where they could live, awaiting the wearing off of the taggant. But I convinced him to let me keep these two cats and that one huge rat with my friends here in the city."

He added upon seeing the quizzical look on my face, "One of those cats, you will notice, is indeed Mrs Hudson's own. The other so identical in appearance, it could very well be its twin and will, with any luck live out the remainder of its life here."

He paused, and sensing that he might be through with his explanation, I pointed out, "But the rat? What on earth could you possibly want with that?"

"Oh, yes" said he. "That is a rather interesting rat. You see as far as I can tell, it never ate any of the taggant altered meat that I sat out on Mrs Hudson's balcony. In fact Lestrade's men picked it up as it was rambling around down by the docks. It is a rather odd specimen, don't you think Watson?" He paused again, this time with a mischievous glint in his eyes.

"And I really am sorry for them giving you such a fright this morning. I forgot to tell you, I kept the remainder of the meat stored in your room."

"They must have somehow discovered it" he said, ending with a smile as our hosts burst out laughing.

Upon The Desk~Cassie Parkes

A cracked skull, once belonging to a man,

Paper, stuffed full of gruesome diagrams,

A magnifying glass, a clock, his violin,

A pair of compasses, some books, some gin.

A human eyeball, how horrid, but more!

A stain of blood, leaking down, to the floor.

Disorganised and horrendously grim,

How peculiar that none of this bothers him!

It is how the man works, how he sees fit

To solve his cases, he would never admit

To any kind of mess or clutter,

Even though Mrs Hudson will mutter

And oh, she'll howl at the mess!

He smiles, saying: "Ah, you digress…"

The Strange Case of Dr. Watson & Mr. Holmes~Jennifer Emerson

I returned to Baker Street after having spent a fortnight on holiday in Scotland in the early morning hours in late October of1886. The autumn chill and the jostling of the hansom on the way home had served to keep me awake. Pausing to pay the cabman and thank him, I put my key into the front door lock.

"Oi, Doc!" a voice whispered.

"Wiggins?" I asked, peering out through the fog. "Is anything wrong?"

"Not with me, Doc," said the boy as he crept closer, "but I don't think Mr. 'olmes has been well."

"Why do you say that, Wiggins?"

"Well, he ain't been 'round much lately, but I seen the lamps burning late into the night."

I looked up and saw that the lamps were still burning.

"What else, Wiggins?"

"Well, 'e were pacing the room; I could see 'im walking back and forth across the window shades. And I heard him talking to someone."

"Wiggins," I sighed, "it was probably just a client."

The boy shook his head vigorously. "Don't think so. See, the queer thing was, no one ever come in or out of the 'ouse." Then he leaned in closer to me. "And it 'appened more than once."

"Thank you for telling me, Wiggins. Leave it to me."

The lad vanished into the night as I opened the front door. Mrs. Hudson was no doubt abed, but the lamps still burning in the sitting room were not unusual for Holmes. So I removed my hat and coat and ascended the familiar seventeen steps.

As I reached the landing, it struck me that perhaps Holmes wouldn't mind a quick chat over a glass of brandy. I was fairly certain I could stay awake that long at least. So I approached the door of the sitting room. But to my surprise, the door was locked.

"Holmes?" I said as I knocked. I became aware of muffled voices coming from the locked room.

"A fine way to welcome a friend back from holiday, Holmes." I called. "Open the door, old man."

"Get rid of him!" a harsh, grating voice exclaimed in a hushed growl.

"He is my trusted colleague—" retorted Holmes.

"If you're as smart as they say you are, you'll tell him to go away!"

The locked turned and the door opened only a crack.

"My dear Watson," whispered Holmes, though I could not see him, "I'm afraid I cannot open the door, as my client requests absolute secrecy."

"But Holmes—"

"I shall explain everything tomorrow. Goodnight."

And with that he closed the door and locked it again. Against my better judgment, I went to bed, but kept my revolver next to me, should I hear my friend call out. I slept well through lunch and up to teatime. Still groggy, I rose and donned my dressing gown. Tea was laid on the table in the sitting room, and I found Mrs. Hudson in the midst of tidying up. The room was practically a shambles.

"So he's been at it again, I see. Another case, Mrs. Hudson?"

"Ha!" she exclaimed. "As if I would know. For the last few weeks he's been more peculiar than ever."

"How do you mean?" I was stunned by her remarks, for Holmes to be acting more peculiar than usual normally foretold of great danger. This case must indeed be singular.

Mrs. Hudson threw up her hands. "I'll get to this later, Doctor. Enjoy your tea, and welcome back."

I smiled. "Thank you, Mrs. Hudson."

Holmes emerged, looking immaculate. Not a hair was out of place, and he positively beamed with energy. He tucked into the food as I have known him to do when a case had been concluded successfully. As if reading my thoughts, Holmes smiled.

"I have no doubt you would care to hear all about it, my dear fellow. However, I regret that this case must not appear in one of your florid tales for the '*Strand Magazine*' My word, Watson; I've not seen you still in your dressing gown at this hour since we first moved in. Pass the butter, would you?"

I handed it to him, "Glad to know I was missed. That's it then?"

"How do you mean, Watson?"

"Aren't you going to deduce the reasons?" I retorted as I reached for the sugar.

His grey eyes twinkled. "Your train was delayed; you were so fatigued that you took no nourishment – which is highly uncharacteristic. I trust you put your revolver away and didn't leave it under your pillow. Mrs. Hudson would have a fit. Really my dear Doctor, you'll come down with something if you keep this up."

I rolled my eyes and took another sip of tea.

He finished his meal, and rose.

"I'm going out, Watson."

"So late in the day?" I answered, "If you'll wait a few moments I'll accompany you."

"No!" he snarled. I paused and watched his expression change in the blink of an eye from rage to regret. His shoulders stooped slightly. "Forgive me, Watson," said Holmes as he ran a trembling hand over his hair, "I didn't sleep well either, and my mind has been greatly vexed of late."

I walked over to him, "Are you sure you're well, my friend?"

"Yes," said Holmes as he donned his top hat, "quite certain. I shan't be long and then I hope you'll do me the honour of joining me by the fire for a brandy this evening."

And with that he left. His outburst had piqued my concern. I knew my friend too well not to sense that something was troubling him. I walked over to his laboratory table. Mrs. Hudson had long ago resigned any responsibility for its tidiness. So I set about straightening it, putting things back in their usual position.

That's when I saw his notebook. Cautiously, I lifted it up. To my horror, I observed that the writing was not his. Indeed, upon closer scrutiny I saw that the entries for the past week and a half were dotted with this strange hand. The latest entry was dated yesterday evening:

...Theory of dual nature of man has been made a reality. Soon I will triumph over Holmes completely. He is no longer necessary...

I nearly dropped the book. How could Holmes not confide in me after five years of harrowing adventures? I read on:

...The Doctor could prove useful...

The horrid thoughts racing in my mind were silenced by a searing pain that coursed through my head. As darkness took me, I heard a familiar voice.

"You couldn't leave well enough alone, could you Watson?"

I woke up bound to my chair at the secretary desk.

"Watson."

I raised my head. It took me a few moments to see through the pain, but I beheld my friend standing at his laboratory table. The table was cluttered with bottles and vials which I did not recognize. His sharp grey eyes, adept at observing even the most insignificant clue, were wide and glazed. I thought at first that he had broken his promise to abstain from the cocaine. But the eyes which were boring into my soul were not his eyes. They were the eyes of a madman.

"Holmes, what have you done?"

He began furiously mixing chemicals.

"I shall show you, Watson."

He produced a strange green mixture and poured it into a glass. I saw him pacing back and forth then he paused before the glass, his mouse-coloured house robe swirling around his legs. He put his hands together in front of his face, as if in prayer. Then he took a deep breath and picked up the glass. He paused, his grey eyes burning as he beheld the liquid inside. He raised the glass to his lips.

"Holmes!"

He screamed and staggered back, his hands clawed at the air, his body twisting and writhing in an unholy fashion. With another shriek he collapsed his head down upon the table, banging his fists and flailing his arms. Bottles crashed all around him as he fell to the floor. Unable to free my bonds. I listened in horror to choking sounds and gasping. Then, silence.

Holmes was still. Too still.

"Holmes! Holmes!" I cried out as I struggled in the ropes. "Answer me!"

Then, one long, bony hand made its way up the table leg. I heard a low sigh as he began to raise himself. I beheld in horror the figure before me. The features of my friend had changed. His hair which only moments ago finely combed, now appeared longer and dishevelled, as if he had stood in the midst of a terrible windstorm. The aquiline face was now sharper and elongated at the nose and chin. His brow had extended forward, creating a hood over large eyes which were now no longer grey, but black. Those lifeless eyes scanned the room, and then rested on me.

"Holmes? Can you hear me?"

He did not reply.

"Do—do you know me?"

"Yes, but you do not know me, Doctor Watson. Mr. Thomas Grey, at your service." His manner was very theatrical, and the sweeping bow he made would have made Sir Henry

Irving envious.

"What?! Holmes, stop this!"

The ghoulish figure before me cackled wildly. "I regret to inform you that Mr. Sherlock Holmes will not returning. But you needn't worry; no harm will come to you. If you do as I ask."

"What do you mean?"

"I need an assistant; someone who can move about in the city. Someone who will not be suspected."

"Never," I answered as I glared back at him.

"Always the shining knight, aren't you? But that can be remedied easily enough."

He poured and mixed chemicals again and poured another glass. The knots held fast yet, I could not free myself! The black eyes widened and shimmered in the dim firelight. He began to laugh maniacally as he twisted his talon-like fingers into my hair and drew back my head and forced the vile to my lips…

"Stop!" I shouted

"Watson, wake up!"

I felt the taste of brandy on my lips, and slowly opened my eyes. Sherlock Holmes knelt before me, clad in his mouse-brown house coat, and looking as he always did.

"That must have been some nightmare indeed, Watson," said my friend as he set the brandy glass down on the nearby table.

"Nightmare?" I said as I looked around me and noticed that all seemed normal.

Holmes reached down and retrieved the book that had fallen to the floor and tapped the cover with the tip of his pipe. "One would think that tonight of all nights a man with your romantic tendencies would have executed more discretion in his choice of books."

He read the title aloud, *"The Strange Case of Dr. Jekyll & Mr. Hyde."* His grey eyes sparkled as he cocked an eyebrow.

"Stevenson again, Watson?" said my friend as he languidly rose and handed me the book.

"Well, I—"

He laughed. "Really, Watson. Drink your brandy. We will

be having company soon."

"Company?"

"Yes," returned my friend as he went into his bedroom. I heard water being poured."The Irregulars are coming by."

"Oh, splendid," I turned and saw the Mrs. Hudson had put out a magnificent repast on the table.

"By the by, Watson," I heard Holmes's voice muffled by a towel, "whatever is that book about?"

He set down the towel and took a black dressing town from his armoire. I rose and filled my pipe from the Persian slipper.

"Uh, never mind, Holmes. Too florid and romantic for you, old man."

His only reply was a snort.

The Holmes Craze Ashley Polasek

(We Didn't Start The Fire by Billy Joel re-imagined....sing along!)

Sherlock Holmes' initial case, Armitage meets his fate
Crown of Stuarts, Ancient rite, Butler silenced

I perceive Afghanistan, just revenge for Jefferson
Stoke Moran, speckled band recoils on the violent

Bum rap for Holder's son, hanging at Trevelyan's
Recoup in the country, murder follows burglary

Cover up at Birlstone, Douglas always on the run
Lord St. Simon's fiancée, blunder in Norbury!

We didn't start the Holmes craze
He's had the world's affection
Since his first detection!

We didn't start the Holmes craze
Though we nurse obsession
With each reading session!

Brother Mycroft, bandaged Greek, periled woman, grinning thief
Agra treasure, Watson's pleasure, River Thames chase

Horse flight, dog at night, everything comes out all right
Cardboard box, Adulterers defaced

The Woman, fast one, Holmes' scheme is all undone

Upper Swandam, building bricks, sleepless smoking, Hugh
Boone's nixed

Step father deceives, wild goose chase, reprieve
Papers gone, vengeance done, Ku Klux Klan in London!

We didn't start the Holmes craze
He's had the world's affection
Since his first detection!

We didn't start the Holmes craze
Though we nurse obsession
With each reading session!

Blackmail, family spat, murderer from Ballarat
Deceit, stolen name, suicide confirms the blame

Brain fever, Tadpole Phelps, sister of the villain helps
Counterfeit printing press, engineer is in distress

Dartmoor demon hound kills, Stapleton's a Baskerville
Justice on Barclay, no French gold for John Clay

Violet Hunter's hair's cropped, faked illness traps the crook
Moriarty! Attack! Plummet down the Reichenbach!

We didn't start the Holmes craze
He's had the world's affection
Since his first detection!

We didn't start the Holmes craze
Though we nurse obsession
With each reading session!

Watson mourns, Holmes back, Colonel Moran trips his trap
War looms, stains prove, Culprit's still in the room

Evidence raises doubt, Fire cry smokes Jonas out
Tyrant, Undone, Cambridge test temptation

Bike ride, forced to wed, Harpoon shot the blackguard dead
Plans astray, hell to pay, what else do I have to say!?

We didn't start the Holmes craze
He's had the world's affection
Since his first detection!

We didn't start the Holmes craze
Though we nurse obsession
With each reading session!

Veiled Lodger, Vampire mum, Staunton's missing from the
scrum
Port crust, only flaw, Sterndale's jungle law
Slaney, Cipher, smell of paint, Milverton's a moral taint
Bonaparte holds Borgia Pearl, Cattle rustling was the clue

Double coffin, Thor Bridge plot, Shoscombe Prince, Watson's
shot
Memoir theft, psychopath, charred face, Lucca's wrath
Leper soldier, Decoy con, Hormone shots turn simian
Lions mane, Impending War, I can't take it anymore!

We didn't start the Holmes craze
He's had the world's affection
Since his first detection!

We didn't start the Holmes craze
Though we nurse obsession
With each reading session!

We didn't start the Holmes craze
But when we are gone it will still go on and on and on and on...

149

A Pleasant Evening~Gemma Richardson

It was a lovely evening Watson thought as he walked down the street. He was heading to Marcini's. It was his favourite place to eat as he enjoyed its peaceful and relaxing atmosphere. Watson was slightly disappointed that Holmes couldn't join him, but he was used to Holmes going off on cases at all times of the day and night. Holmes had been busy on this particular case for several days now and Watson knew very little about what his friend was up to. Mrs Hudson had told Watson that she would not step inside Holmes's room until he had cleared up his mess. Holmes was frequently throwing things about the place, not really caring where they ended up. He still hadn't repaired the wall where he had shot several bullets into it in the form of the letters VR. It took two weeks to calm Mrs Hudson down after that particular episode.   Watson stepped in through the door and walked to the bar.

"Hello there, what can I get you?" asked the bartender.

"I'll have a whiskey please," said Watson.

Watson noticed a lady standing to his left. She was in a long dark red dress and had blonde hair flowing down her back. He couldn't help but look at her. Her dark brown eyes shone and her lips were a full deep red.

"Yes?" she asked.

"Oh I'm sorry, how rude of me. My name is John Watson"

"Frances Mayweather," she replied.

The bartender returned with his drink.

"Thank you," said Watson taking a sip.

"Are you eating in?" asked the bartender.

"Would you like to join me?" Watson asked, looking at Frances.

"Yes, why not, thank you Mr Watson."

"It's Doctor, actually."

The bartender led them to a table and took their order. Watson and Frances talked as they ate, discussing recent news and events happening in London.

"Am I right in assuming you are the same Doctor Watson that lives with Mr Sherlock Holmes, am I right?" asked Frances changing the subject.

"Yes I am. Why do you ask?"

"I merely wondered. What's he like?"

"Now that's a question," said Watson smiling at the thought of his friend.

"What do you mean?" asked Frances, looking puzzled yet intrigued.

"I suppose you could say Holmes is unique. He's intelligent and quick witted. A great detective in every way. He doesn't seek fame and fortune in what he does. But he does have his strange habits. I can't stand his addiction to drugs either, unfortunately nothing I say to him seems to sink in."

"Do you regret moving in with him?"

"Oh of course not, not for a second. He might test my patience every now and then, but I'd never want to leave Baker Street."

"He sounds like a good man."

"Yes he is," said Watson.

They finished their meal, talked a little more before leaving Marcini's. Watson hailed a cab for Frances.

"It was nice meeting you. Maybe we should meet up again sometime," said Watson as he held out a hand.

"Yes it was a lovely evening, thank you. Well I know where you live so I'll send you a letter."

Frances climbed into the carriage and waved to Watson as it pulled away. Watson felt slightly sad that such a wonderful evening had to end. He made his way slowly back to Baker Street.

Watson stepped through the front door and hung his coat and hat on the stand. It was late and he assumed that Mrs Hudson had gone to bed. He quietly made his way upstairs and saw the light was still on in the living room. He wondered if Holmes had stayed up until he had come home, but he dismissed that thought as it wasn't something Holmes would do. Watson opened the door and walked in. Holmes wasn't in the room, but Watson could see Holmes's bedroom door was still open and the light on. Suddenly Watson noticed a dress hanging up on the door and it looked remarkably familiar.

"Holmes?" asked Watson cautiously.

He moved forward and looked around the corner into Holmes' room. There standing in front of his mirror was Holmes. He was wearing one of his night gowns, but his hair was different indeed. He removed the long blonde wig from his head and placed it onto the table beside him. He took a wet sponge to his face and wiped off the makeup.

"Holmes ..." Watson's voice trailed off as it dawned on him what Holmes had been up to that evening.

Holmes so absorbed in what he was doing he hadn't noticed Watson come in. But he defiantly heard the thump behind him. Watson was lying on the floor having fainted from what he just saw.

"Oh, Watson. You weren't supposed to see this."

Holmes poured a glass of whiskey and knelt at his friend's side waiting for him to stir. After a few minutes Watson opened his eyes to see Holmes there with an apologetic smile and a glass of whiskey. He sat up and took a sip. When he gathered up some strength he muttered to Holmes

"How could you to this to me, Holmes?"

"I'm really sorry Watson. I wasn't expecting you to arrive tonight. I was working on a case."

"But why didn't you say anything?"

"I didn't want to ruin my cover. I can't say how sorry I am."

"You even asked me about what I thought of you!"

"Sorry I couldn't help myself," said Holmes smiling.

The Boys from Baker Street~Grace Smoczyk

There are two boys from Baker Street;

To meet them would be quite the treat!

But alas! That cannot be,

For they lived long ago, you see.

But for those who love them well,

Of them, we can tell!

I am one of these,

So listen well if you please!

One 'boy' is tall and dark

On your life, he'll leave a mark.

He is full of mischief and fun,

But puts villains on the run

For he is also terribly smart,

And pretends not to have a heart.

But we know better, of course,

And can feel no remorse.

With the power of his mind he can show the way,

Show the way, and save the day.

He helps those with needs,

And performs great deeds.

Deeds of daring and might-

Thrusting him to great height

For his name goes down throughout history,

As the supreme solver of mystery.

Mention his name, and criminals shake

For with that name, their fears awake.

He is ever here, with truth and judgment in his hand,

Bringing justice throughout all the land.

Sherlock Holmes is his name,

And to the world he came.

A role to fill, a destiny to complete,

To perform the most daring feat;

To help the helpless, both rich and poor

For his help, people came from every shore.

A hero, a legend, alone he stands,

A model of greatness to all lands.

With jet black hair and eyes of grey,

He's a hero, here to stay.

But where would our hero be without his one true friend-

The one with him to the end?

Dr. John Watson: kind and true

Loyal throughout the dangers they go through.

Lovable and smart; though somewhat dim,

Patiently putting up with Sherlock's whim.

He is the other 'boy' from Baker Street,

This dangerous duo, no criminal can beat!

So villains beware,

Cross these two-if you dare!

They have no age, they're always here,

Perhaps that is why they are so dear.

So now you see why it would be a treat,

To meet the 'boys' from Baker Street!

Family~Carolanne Roe

The sitting room door of 221B Baker Street was thrust open vigorously, making a loud thud against the wall behind. Sherlock Holmes came strolling through purposefully and began removing his hat, gloves and coat without even looking up.

"Watson, my good man." He called into the sitting room. "I have been at the mortuary all day! You will not believe what I have discovered about the post mortem bruising process…"

Holmes was stopped mid-sentence by Watson rising from his chair by the fire place. A middle aged woman rose from the couch opposite, a small boy remained on the floor playing with some wooden toys. The woman looked a little green as she faced Holmes outburst with a rather strained smile.

"Holmes," Watson said. "This is Mrs Elizabeth Crowley." Holmes extended his hand to the well-dressed Lady. "…nee Watson," he continued.

Holmes eyes darted to Watson standing by his side. He managed to contain his shock slightly. He did not think there was a lot the mild mannered Dr Watson could do to shock him. Holmes eyes then darted to the floor where the child was sitting. Same sandy coloured hair as the Doctor, a familiarity in the facial structure, eye colour both green, ear lobe development similar…Holmes forced a strained smile. "A pleasure to meet you madam," he said, smoothly.

Holmes indicated back to the chair she had just vacated while he threw his outer clothing items into a corner and sat himself in a chair by the fire place. It unfortunately put the child at his feet. "What brings you to Baker Street, Mrs Crowley?"

"Well I came to visit John, Mr Holmes. It has been a while since me or Hamish has seen him and he has very kindly agreed to a small favour." Holmes could only assume 'Hamish' was the John H. Watson look-a-like sitting on the floor.

Watson smirked inwardly at his friend's nonplussed expression .For once he had the upper hand. Holmes had used his superbly, brilliant, calculating, clinical mind, put two and two together and came up with five! He had better put him out his misery.

"Beth is my brother's widow, Holmes, but has since re-married. The boy, my brother's son, is my nephew."

"Your brother was married?" Holmes asked.

"Didn't get THAT from the pocket watch did you" Watson gloated as he smirked across at his friend, who simply raised an eyebrow, but pursed his lips.

Holmes turned back to Beth. "So, my dear. What is this favour you are in need of from the good doctor? No doubt Watson has informed you of my work and I would be happy to assist in any problem you may have."

"Oh, that is very kind of you Mr Holmes but John hasn't really talked about you much while I have been here."

Watson grinned inwardly, 'that'll be a blow to his ego'.

"But I am aware of your great work, sir, as I do read the published journal entries John has written about your adventures together. I must say they sound so fascinating!"

Holmes face clouded. "Cases, madam, cases, *not* adventures, I am a consulting detective, not a treasure hunter," he replied icily.

"Beth has many errands to run in London, Holmes, as she lives in Inverness and has had a long and tiring journey. I have offered to look after Hamish for a few hours, possibly the night, to give her time to accomplish all her tasks before she returns home by train tomorrow. It will keep him out from under her feet for a while at least." He smiled jovially and leaned down towards the boy. "What do you say Hamish? A few hours with your Uncle John eh? We will have some fun, won't we lad?"

The boy smiled back up at the group. "Yes Uncle! I am I going to stay here?" He asked excitedly.

"Of course" Watson replied cutting off Holmes smoothly,

just as he was about to open his mouth with a possible objection.

"Really, Watson!" Holmes finally interrupted, a little angrily. "I have vital work to do, there are important experiments lying all around the sitting room! Baker Street is not place for a child!"

Beth looked uneasy then glanced around the rather messy room and began having second thoughts, some of those stories… "Well, I must say John; I think Mr Holmes may be right. If it is too dangerous to leave him here…"

"Nonsense!" Watson interjected. "He will be just fine. If I haven't managed to kill myself with all Holmes's toxic experiments over the years then the boy will be fine as well for one night." Watson chuckled at his own joke.

After perhaps a half hour of further idle chit chat, Dr Watson escorted Elizabeth downstairs then called upon Mrs Hudson for some help in setting out space in his room where his nephew could sleep for the night. Holmes, glad to be alone once more, was sitting at his desk absorbed in mixing the correct quantities of chemicals for one of his experiments. He became acutely aware of a small presence standing just over his left shoulder. He turned around in his chair fully and looked at the boy.   "Yes?"Holmes enquired.

"What are you doing?" Hamish asked, craning around Holmes to look at the items stretched out on the work bench.

"Working!" Was the detective's rather short reply.

"Oh…." Then, "On what?"

"I am attempting to ascertain whether the residue I discovered on the body I examined day before last is in fact, gunpowder."

"And is it?"

Holmes sighed irritably. "I do not know yet as I have not finished the test."

"Can I try?"

"No."

"Why not?" The boy asked rather petulantly.

"The experiment is very delicate, it is not for children."

Hamish pursed his lips. "It does not look particularly

difficult."

"Watson!" Holmes suddenly called. No answer. "Watson!"

Watson appeared at the door of the sitting room. "Yes, Holmes?"

Holmes shot Watson a withering look that spoke volumes. The good doctor noticed his nephew leaning over Holmes work desk absorbed in probing the contents of jars.

"Err…" Watson stammered. "Hamish. Why don't you get your coat on and we shall go out for a walk and some fresh air."

"Can we ride in a hansom, Uncle?" Hamish asked excitedly.

"Of course we can." Watson smiled and went to fetch his coat from upstairs. Holmes returned to his experiment satisfied he would now get peace and quiet. However a small voice in his left ear suddenly startled him from his work.

"Are you coming too, sir?"

"No, I am not coming with you and your uncle."

"Why not?"

Holmes silently counted to ten. "Because I have important work to do."

"Oh." Then, "It's not very much though, is it? That can't possibly take you all day."

"I have other things to do besides this."

Hamish smiled, interested. "Like what?"

"It is of no concern of yours."

"But I am interested!"

"Do you always ask so many questions?" Holmes finally asked, exasperated.

"Are you always so unforthcoming when answering questions?"The boy replied.

He thought for a moment before replying, "Yes. It is my job to question, not to be questioned"

Hamish nodded in understanding, but continued his vigil of looking across Holmes's shoulder.

"Can I try?" He finally began again.

Holmes voice became threateningly low. "I have already

said no."

"Please?"

Holmes took a deep breath and remained silent, trying to focus on his work. After a few more strained silent minutes Watson appeared at the sitting room door dressed for outdoors.

"Come on Hamish" He called. "Put your coat on and we are ready to go."

"Bye" The boy called behind him as he headed for the door. "See you later."

"Not if I can help it." Holmes muttered under his breath as he heard the click of the sitting room door closing.

Deductions~Cassie Parkes

Calloused hands? A writer.

Scuffed up knuckles? A fighter.

Paint flecks on clothes? An artist.

A stench of chemicals? A scientist.

Stains of brown around the lips? A drinker of teas.

Honeycombs upon the shoes? A keeper of bees.

Pin needle pricks? A seamstress.

Bite marks and bruises? A mistress.

So simple. But what of those who are kind, and loyal, and constant?

That deduction is nearer to home.

A friend. The friend, of course. Just the one.

Holmes from Home~Carolanne Roe

The sky directly above me is grey and an angry grey at that, the large manor-like building directly in front; grey also. I have the feeling it is rubbing off on my mood and can certainly feel one of my depressions coming on. I begin walking up to the polished, dark wooden door, looking for signs of life and any movements within the house or in the surrounding grounds. The gravel crunches under my feet as I cross the neatly trimmed lush green lawns and pebbled walkways. The front door is already open; welcoming me in.

Inside is surprisingly light given the gloom outside but no amount of brightness can mask the smell, it attacks my nostrils the instant I step in from the cool air outside; disinfectant. A smell I know only too well with an underlying smell of, what? Staleness, I conclude. Oh, don't get me wrong the interior is clean, spotlessly so in fact. Although the furnishings may seem a little worn or the carpet slightly threadbare at patches, I observe all surfaces have been scrubbed and polished within an inch of their lives.

I wander across the spacious hallway, intent on my destination. I have been here many times before, I know my way around well. I nod to the girl passing on my left, she smiles warmly back at me then goes back to her chores of polishing the brass ornamentation. I don't think it needs it but she is unlikely to defer to my assurance that the brassware has seen quite enough polishing for one lifetime. As I pass through the threshold of the reception into the next main room, the heat attacks my senses. Two fire places are light and the flames dance merrily. Two fires? It is the middle of August! A small bead of sweat forms at my hairline and trickles down my back to my collar. I remove my light outer coat and unfasten my inner jacket to relieve the stuffiness around my person.

The room I have entered is large and cavernous but conservatively decorated. Aside from the two fireplaces burning away there are a number of high backed chairs scattered throughout, with small tables nestles beside them. I spot the large fading red chair in the far right hand corner of the room; my goal. The chair has its back to me, the front facing outward through the large glass doors leading outside to the rear of the property and overlooking the gardens. Outside I can see a few elderly people wandering through the lawns, sitting by the flowers or even reading beside the fountain.

I approach the chair and take my usual position in the smaller, green-leather, wing backed chair a little to its left. He is there, as he always is, as I expected him to be, looking to the outside. I put down my bag and walking stick at the side of my chair and sit myself comfortably.

"Good morning my good man. How are you today?" I enquire.

My friend turns from his survey on the outside to look at me. I smile brightly and he returns it, although a little more hesitantly. Something in his look tells me and I know he is wondering who I am.

"I am fine thank you, and yourself?" is his polite response. He goes back to gazing out of the window. He looks tired and frail, I must admit. He is not a small man but the high backed chair seems to engulf him and age has taken its toll. Despite the season and fullness of the hearth a small tartan blanket is draped over his lap obscuring part of the suit he is wearing. I notice he has been impeccably well dressed this morning, probably as they known he will have visitors.

I reach down and pull a few books put of my bag. "I have brought you some books. They are some of your favourites. I thought you might like them to look later."

"That is very kind of you" he says, absently.

I place the books on the small table sitting next to his chair. The table already contains a large stack of papers, some

165

reading glasses and a glass of water. I pull off the top most newspaper and open it out examining the front page.

"Oh ho!" I cry, "How about the news of that burglary from the London Museum, eh? Got away with a priceless painting it says here." I comment, attempting to engage his interest. He turns back to me.

"I am sorry, my mind was elsewhere. You were saying something?"

"Yes, the burglary" I say and point to the newspaper.

"Ah." Was his only response. Then "I'm sorry but… who are you?"

My heart hits the floor. I try not to betray my feelings in my response. "Holmes! It's Watson." I say with a small laugh and a bright smile, looking directly at him.

His eyes shine with pleasure. Dawning comprehension fills him as he turns fully in his chair to look at me. "Watson!" He cries. "My dear fellow, how have you been?"

"Fine" I reply, "just fine, Holmes."

"I have not seen you in ages."

This is not true, of course, but it is best to let it lie.

"And how is…and how is M-Mary?"

My mouth opens but no sound manages to come out. It is a few moments before I can say "Mary passed away, Holmes…remember?"

He looked shocked "No! When?"

"Before your travels in Tibet." I sighed inwardly, we had been here before. He narrowed his eyes in concentration.

"Tibet? Moriarty tried to kill me."

"Yes, Holmes."

"We were too good for him you and I, Watson. Moriarty and Moran, we got them all." My friend steepled his fingers in front of his nose and shot me a mischievous glance out the corner of his eyes. He chuckled, a deep throaty sound. You would almost think he was back to his old self.

"Gave you quite a start in your waiting room when I returned didn't I, Watson?"

I grinned at him recalling how overjoyed I was to see him

again after three long years of mourning his loss at Reichenbach. The mere shock of seeing him come back from the dead rendered me unconscious.

"You did indeed."

We chatted idly on various things for several hours. We light a pipe or two and reminisced over some old times with myself filling in the ever increasing blanks in his memory and occasionally having to repeat myself ; we must have gone over the details of the Gloria Scott at least three times this afternoon, but I didn't mind one bit, this was a good day. All that was missing was a small brandy for each of us. I wondered if I could sneak a small flask in next time as a rare treat.

After a period I could tell he was tiring. His responses were not as detailed and our chat was becoming punctuated by long periods of silence with Holmes staring out the windows into the garden.

"Would you like to go out into the garden for a while, Holmes?" I asked, looking outside. Small rays of sunshine were threatening to break through the cloudy sky. Perhaps the fresh air would do him a little good, as I always said. Although a little unsteady on my own feet with a few age-related health problems I am sure I could steer him through a few laps of the garden successfully.

"No thank you," was his reply. "I m a little tired. I think I will just sit in this chair for a while." His mood and speech suddenly changed, ever so slightly. "Anyway, I have a client due to arrive at any moment. A young lady has a problem with a disappearing fiancé."

"I-I don't think you will have clients coming here, Holmes." I tried my best to let him down gently.

"Nonsense. Two O'clock is the appointment, Watson."

I let the matter rest. In all likelihood he would now doze in his armchair for a while before dinner was served then one of the carers would come to get him ready for bed.

"Well, I must be going." I said checking my watch. "I will come see you again Holmes. "

I rose from my chair patting him gently on the shoulder. "Goodbye for now."

As I get up I deposit the paper back onto of the pile. He gives me a slight wave as I pick up my coat, bag and walking stick and edge around the chair heading for the door, but his expression is more than a little vague.

I will come see him again same time next week, as usual, as always.

Loss~Jane Stuart

A pocket watch: a past concealed;

Its features, closely studied, yield

A history from each commonplace,

Well-worn and battered mark and trace.

A brother's grief and loss revealed.

~o~

No fifty guinea watch can shield

The truth and nothing can replace

The words unsaid and wounds unhealed.

A pocket watch.

~o~

The power which drink and debt can wield

Ensured his brother's fate was sealed.

Four numbers, scratched inside the case,

Count down a tragic fall from grace.

Memento from a battlefield;

A pocket watch.

Company~Jane Stuart

(POV of Watson; Christmas Eve)

He hears the final patient bid farewell and close the door;

It's only half past eight; he'd hoped for several clients more.

As long as he is busy, useful, fully occupied;

He can, perhaps, forget who should be standing at his side.

He wishes his assistant all the best for Christmas day;

Then turns, and lets his calm physician's mask just fall away.

He hears the background chatter of the world outside his door;

Amazed that London life goes on exactly as before.

His grief has disconnected him from every day routine:

His current life; his hoped-for life; the chasm in between.

~0~

No Christmas decorations; not a hint of festive cheer;

No cause to celebrate, with those he loved no longer here.

~0~

Prescriptions checked, equipment cleared, a solitary meal.

A doctor who could not predict when wounds would start to heal

He sits, with stacks of BMJs, and reads by candle light;

Prepared, from past experience, for one more sleepless night.

He glances at two objects, put so carefully in place;

A blue-eyed smiling portrait and a battered silver case.

~0~

At midnight, there's a gentle, nervous tapping at the door;

He finds a group of urchins he's met many times before.

They tumble in; a jostling crowd of short humanity:

Young Wiggins tells the doctor that he needs their company.

They settle in his sitting room; on cushions, floor and chair;

Announcing they have stories they would really like to share.

They talk of Holmes adventures and the foes they helped defeat:

The doctor feels, for one short hour, he's back in Baker Street.

The urchins then head out; they leave a gift; a Christmas tree:

A branch, if truth be told; fir cones and rags, strung carefully.

~0~

Another hour; another knock; the door is opened wide:

Two Yarders, Hopkins and Lestrade, stand patiently outside.

They tell him, they were passing and they saw the candle light

And wondered if the doctor wanted company that night.

Invited in; they sit back with an offered drink in hand;

And recall those baffling cases which were published in "The Strand".

The doctor finds himself engrossed in familiar tales of old;

Those days when he had Holmes to help, and Mary's hand to hold.

An hour flies by; the Yarders stand to leave; just one thing more:

A slightly battered holly wreath to hang upon the door.

~0~

The doctor sleeps a little, waking up before the dawn;

And wonders how he'll fill a bleak and empty Christmas morn.

~o~

A knock; a stranger at the door; well dressed; smart hat and coat:

A covered basket in his hand; a neatly written note.

A Christmas lunch from Mycroft; freshly cooked, from his hotel.

A reminder there were others who were missing Holmes as well.

He thanks the man politely; puts the basket to one side;

Touched by this thoughtful gesture, on a lonely Christmastide.

~0~

And finally, mid morning, there is one more Christmas guest;

The faithful Mrs. Hudson, calm as always, warmly dressed.

She knows just what the doctor needs: a Christmas morning walk:

Sherlock Holmes and Mary Morstan; she can listen; he can talk.

And he does; they stroll together through the crisp clear winter frost

And he tells her how it's really been since both of them were lost.

His words at first are hesitant; this is not his usual role;

He's the one who calmly listens while another bares his soul.

He's the sidekick or physician, with a notebook in his hand;

Not the client, nor the patient; but begins to understand.

He remains the same John Watson; still in mourning; dignified;

But something, very slowly, is unknotting, deep inside.

~o~

There's no quick and easy method which will mend a broken heart;

He knows his friends are there to watch his back;

And that's a start.

Polycephaly~Vida Starčević

He comes back from Switzerland a few days after the event, having checked all possible sources for traces of his friend, until he is finally certain that nothing has remained of him but a scrap of paper stuffed under a rock. There is no body to bury, only a handful of his notes that he makes sure are stowed away safely in his case. Along with this, there is a pair of cufflinks that he was given by a grateful client, but that he never wore. He puts the box with the cufflinks in the inside pocket of his jacket: he wants to make sure that they don't get lost on the journey back.

The first couple of weeks are confusing and difficult: he plans to sort through all of his dead friend's papers, which turns out to be far more taxing work than he originally thought. The housekeeper is no help, and the filing system his friend had been using proves to be almost indecipherable to him. In the end, he opts for sitting in his friend's armchair through the night, cigarette in hand, poring over notebook after file after bits of foolscap tied together with pieces of frayed string, all scrawled thoroughly with his friend's sometimes barely legible handwriting.   He goes through more cups of tea in those weeks than he had in his entire term of serving in the army, when the only point of comfort in a dark, foreign place was a warm cup of something that tasted almost entirely unlike the stuff he drank at home, but the fumes of which were familiar enough to remind him of the country he yearned to go back to. Walking the streets of London to meet up with a friend or an old client is a vastly different affair now.

Although he was always used to carrying out certain meetings without his friend, he was always conscious of the fact that he would need to report to him at the end of the day. His presence was
there in his mind, regardless of the fact that they might not have walked in step with each other; now, he knows that the only person he answers to is himself, and the sensation is new and unwelcome, like snow fallen down the back of his jacket, or hot ashes flicked on the skin of his hand.

Sometimes, he thinks he sees his friend's face, in the crowd on Piccadilly Circus, or strolling next to the boating lake at Regent's Park, but when he looks closer he realises that the shape of the man's nose or the line of his jaw is entirely different, and the hopeful shout of his friend's name dies on his lips.

He goes to dinner at his club after a long while of solitary dining in his friend's old sitting room, the same room where they saw clients and discussed problems, although he was just as content to merely listen to his friend's monologues. He fixes the chain of his pocket watch and smoothes out his suit in the mirror. The man staring back at him is much different than he was ten years ago, when he and his friend first came across each other. Then, he was fresh out of the army, shoulders still stiff
with discipline, hair cropped close and moustache trimmed to regulation. Now that it is 1891, the moustache remains as diligently maintained as ever, but the man behind it has aged. The area
around his eyes is beginning to display the first signs of crow's feet, and the laugh lines become etched deeper into his skin every time he smiles. A corner of his mouth quirks into a grin and he reaches for his friend's old cufflinks which are already waiting for him, snug in their box on the mantelpiece. He secures them to the cuffs of his freshly starched shirt.

Once at the club he sits alone, although more than one face looks up at him hoping to be asked to dine with him. He knows them all by name, and he has played cards and shared pipe smoke with most of them, but he does not hold them in very high regard. They are men who seem to be almost permanently

installed at the club, to such a degree that only the fact that they move and breathe
keeps them off the club's inventory lists.

He orders beef Wellington, rare, and gets a glass of wine with his cigarette as he waits for his food.
Feeling comfortably idle in the familiar surroundings, he raises his eyes from his wine at the same time that a man a few tables down from him looks up from lighting his pipe. A cold dread runs through his blood as he recognises the right-hand man of the villain who caused the death of his friend. For a moment, their eyes lock, and the man looks mortified. He is probably experiencing the same thing: how could he find me here, the place where I thought I was safe from this kind of intrusion? A waiter approaches the man and blocks him from view.

He takes a deep drag on his cigarette. The man might as well have pulled out a gun and aimed it between his eyes for the effect that simply catching a glimpse of him across a room has on him. His palms are clammy; his heart is racing as he remembers having to go back to his lodgings when he was halfway to the club because he had forgotten his money. Taking his gun did not even cross his mind. Keeping his face impassive, he gets up from his table, motioning to the waiter, who immediately slinks away from the man. He crosses the room, reaching the man just as he is whipping his napkin from his lap onto the table, trying to be as quick as possible to leave. He claps a hand on the man's shoulder, gently but firmly, and the man slumps back down into his chair.

"Don't get up, Doctor Watson," he says to the man. "Won't we have dinner like gentlemen?"

"I see no gentleman here," Watson says brusquely.

"I'm having the beef Wellington, myself," he says, ignoring the doctor's remark and sitting opposite him. "Although I have heard that the curry they are offering is equally as good. It's a bit too fashionable for me. I'm very much a traditionalist when it comes to my food."

"I didn't say you could join me," scoffs Watson.

"Surely you wouldn't deny an old army chum?"

"We never served together."

"Ah, yes," he concedes, "you were in the 66th Berkshires, is that right? A very brave regiment. Everyone still talks about the great hero of Maiwand, Bobbie. He made his way all the fifty miles back to Kandahar, did you know? He even got awarded a medal from the Queen herself, until he met his untimely demise under the wheels of a London cab. Quite remarkable, really," he says."For a dog," he adds with a smile.

He pauses as the waiter brings over his beef Wellington and Watson's curry with steamed rice. He smirks at the dish, and raises his glass of wine towards the doctor. "I propose a toast. For the brave staff of your field hospital in Afghanistan, who fled leaving the wounded behind or got drunk in the officers' mess, and only survived because they were slung over horses: that is, if they were sober enough to stay on. Here's to them." He raises his glass to his lips and drinks.

Watson does not touch his. "What do you want from me, Colonel?" he demands.

"From you? Nothing. I went out tonight with the single purpose to have dinner at my club. I had no idea you would be here as well. But I do suggest you start eating before it gets cold. You wouldn't want to offend the chef."

Watson appears to regard him for a second, eyebrows raised, and then he picks up his fork, stabbing it violently into the curry, and tucks in. With an almost imperceptible grin, the colonel starts carving his own beef.

They eat in silence for a while, the only sounds the scraping of their forks against their plates and the regular background noises of the club: men laughing, glasses chinking, evening newspapers being ruffled, and the occasional burp.

"My wife knows I'm here, you know," Watson says after a while, mixing the rice on his plate with the remainder of the curry sauce. "She will alert the police if I don't come back."

"Were you planning on spending the night somewhere other than your wife's bed?" Watson looks taken aback by this, his fork stalled halfway to his mouth. "I am not going to kill you.

I have very little quarrel with you, and I am sure you don't have a lot against me."

"But you're – you were Moriarty's second-in-command," he argues. "I've seen Holmes's notes about you. Sebastian Moran, the second most dangerous man in London!"

"Do keep your voice down, Doctor, I don't want people to get jealous," drawls Moran, idly picking at the salmon roe. "And for your information, I didn't get to where I am without a well-honed sense of self-preservation. I wouldn't simply pull my gun on a man in my own club. My methods are far more," he pauses, considering this, and ends with, "discreet."

"We've exposed Moriarty, Holmes and I," says Watson, sounding more self assured. "Lestrade has assured me that there have been over a dozen arrests made since I returned from Meiringen. Your organisation has been found out; it's collapsing like a house of cards. Soon no amount of discretion will save you from gaol."

"You think you've cut off the snake's head? Let me tell you something." Moran sets his fork down on his now empty plate, wiping pastry crumbs off his moustache. He leans forwards ever so slightly, regarding the doctor intently.

"Hercules fought the Lernaean Hydra, and when he cut one head off, he found that two immediately took its place. The moral of the story is: don't start a battle you can't win, Doctor Watson."

Watson pushes his plate away towards the centre of the table. He takes a sip of his wine, and sets the glass down, twirling the stem between thumb and forefinger. Moran considers him quietly. They are not all too unlike: the only way in which they differ is their former rank and the side of the law they operate on. They have both worked for, and been the best friends of, two of the brightest minds of their generation. After witnessing their deaths, they have both tried to return to their daily lives and pick up the pieces, repair the web, tug at old threads and spin new ones. He catches himself wondering if the necktie Watson is wearing used to belong to Holmes: it is an ill match for his eyes, but it looks well-worn.

Abruptly, Watson lets go of his wine glass and stands up. "You forget one thing, Colonel," he says, and when he uses Moran's rank it sounds like an insult. "Hercules did beat the monster. The Hydra only had one immortal head, and he cut it off with a golden sword given to him by the goddess of wisdom." Watson relights his pipe. "I would keep one eye open for the glitter of gold, if I were you."

He gives the colonel a curt nod and briskly leaves the table, leaving behind only the smell of pipe smoke.

Moran chuckles to himself, and beckons the waiter over to order a bottle of port before his regular evening game of whist. He silently toasts to the doctor's good health.

He does not see Doctor Watson for another three years. When he does, he is kneeling on the floor of Camden House, rifle in hand. The weapon is pointed at the sitting room window of 221B Baker Street, and he has the silhouette of Sherlock Holmes in his sights, aiming right between his eyes. After pulling the trigger, after feeling that rush of excitement and pride he always gets following a successful kill, he is knocked to the floor by John Watson, and as Sherlock Holmes stands above him, smiling in the half-light, Sebastian Moran thinks he sees a flicker of gold as Athena's sword hits home.

Parrot Fashion~David Ruffle

With the assistance and know-how of Melody Ruffle.

Of course I should have known better, I really should. Having been an intimate friend of the renowned and celebrated Mr Sherlock Holmes for so long, I should have realised how it would end. But here I am telling my story hindmost first as Holmes would say, one of my faults it seems.

"What is it," asked Holmes one morning as I returned to our rooms with a large object covered with an old pair of curtains.

"Let me show you," I exclaimed and pulled away the curtains, revealing a large bird cage.

"What is it," asked Holmes again.

"It's a bird cage."

` "Thank you," he said with some asperity, "I had managed to deduce that fact for myself. "What is the creature that appears to be residing in it?"

"A parrot, Holmes." I replied somewhat impatiently.

"You astound me my dear fellow, but once again I had deduced that fact also, perhaps my question to you should have been, why, why is it here?"

"A grateful patient, Sir Oscar Oliver-Onyx gave him to me in gratitude for my medical services to his family."

"All very worthy I am sure, but why is it, he or she here in our quarters?"

"You would hardly expect me to keep *her* in my bedroom surely."

"I would not expect you to keep her anywhere in these quarters. Whatever would Mrs Hudson say? I have no doubt we will be given notice to quit."

"Mrs Hudson is quite taken with Angel actually."

"Angel?" queried Holmes with one raised eyebrow.

"She needs a name, Holmes, just the same as any pet."

"So you can call her when you take her for a walk in the park?! If Mrs Hudson is so taken with Angel perhaps she will not object to having this parrot in her kitchen or failing that.......the cellar!"

Sherlock Holmes was not enamoured of the notion of keeping pets, my long lost bull-pup could testify to that. He tolerated dogs as working animals, at least those of the species who could follow a scent. I decided to approach the problem of Angel from a scientific viewpoint.

"This parrot is a Blue Crowned Conure, a very intelligent member of this sub-species. It can be taught to talk if one has the patience to do so, perhaps it may be that they can be useful as witnesses to a crime and be able to bring perpetrators to book through identification of the same and revealing what they have heard or seen."

"I feel you are getting into the realms of fantasy there and you have to recognise there is a huge difference between speech and mere mimicry which is all these birds can manage. You are no doubt aware of the expression 'bird-brain'?"

"Regardless of your objections, Angel will be remaining here and I will be involving myself in the matter of her *education*."

"So be it, Watson."

My efforts over the ensuing weeks were concentrated, but fruitless, not a word would she utter. I reasoned it may be a matter of trust and I did everything in my power to make her comfortable. I purchased the best seed and nut mix; I kept her supplied with fruit and vegetables that would have graced any table. Twice a day I released her from the confines of her cage so she could fly around the rooms at will. Holmes encouraged me to do this, but only when he was absent because Angel seemed to find Holmes's head a favourite perch.

"Hello. Hello. Hello. Who's a pretty girl then? Hello Angel. Hello......."

"Watson, Watson, please desist."

"Angel needs mental stimulation, Holmes, it's essential for her well-being."

"And this she gets from you?"

"Yes, as she is going to get precious little from you in that regard. You could regard her as a challenge to be met and then rise to that challenge. Hello. Hello. Hello. Hello Angel....."

"I think I will go for a stroll and leave you to it, I sense a real battle of wits shaping up here," he said, laughing.

In spite of Holmes's words I felt a cooling of his animosity towards Angel and he certainly took his part in the feeding and flying routine, even to the point of allowing her to perch on his shoulder (he drew a line regarding his head being used as such).
However bizarre it may sound I often found Holmes and Angel together by the fire with what seemed like conspiratorial looks and glance between them. What ineffable twaddle I told myself.

Sometime later I had been out for a constitutional one morning, when I entered our sitting-room I was greeted with:

"Good morning, Doctor Watson."

It was Angel. I could scarcely believe my ears, but I suspected that my efforts had been in vain and that another had taken a hand.

"Great God in Heaven, Holmes, how did you do it?"

I looked from Angel to Holmes and back. I saw one mouth open, I saw one beak open and even as they spoke in unison, I knew the words they would utter.

"It was elementary, my dear Watson," they chorused.

Plaudits and Bouquets

My thanks go to... Mike B, Jennifer, Vida, Jane, Mike, Cassie, Jane, Paula, Ashley, Carolanne, David, Gemma, Jane, Grace, 'Singular', Mike W and Melody for graciously allowing me permission to use their work and even more graciously, for allowing me to tamper with them (the works not the contributors themselves!)

We are all grateful for the creators and moderators of Holmesian.net for maintaining the forum which encouraged nearly every one of us to dabble.

My personal thanks go to all my fellow contributors here for their friendship and encouragement.

Thanks, once more to Steve and Bob for allowing the book you are holding now to come to life.

David Ruffle.

Also from MX Publishing

  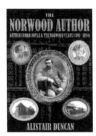 

Four books on Sir Arthur Conan Doyle by Alistair Duncan including a an overview of all the stories (**Eliminate The Impossible**), a London guide (**Close to Holmes**), the winner of the Howlett Award 2011 (**The Norwood Author**) and the book on Undershaw (**An Entirely New Country**).

Short fiction collections from Tony Reynolds (**Lost Stories of Sherlock Holmes**), Gerard Kelly (**The Outstanding Mysteries of Sherlock Holmes**) and Bertram Fletcher Robinson (**Aside Arthur Conan Doyle**).

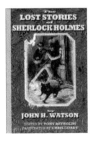  

www.mxpublishing.com

Also From MX Publishing

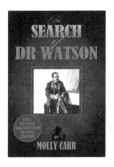
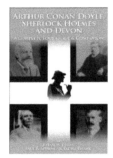

A biography (**In Search of Dr Watson**), a travel guide (**Sherlock Holmes and Devon**), a novel where Sherlock Holmes battles The Phantom (**Rendezvous at The Populaire**), a novel featuring Dr. Watson (**Watson's Afghan Adventure**), a fantasy novel (**Shadowfall**) and an intriguing collection of papers from The Hound (**The Official Papers Into The Matter Known as The Hound of The Baskervilles**).

www.mxpublishing.com

Also From MX Publishing

Two 'Female Sherlock Holmes' novels (**The Sign of Fear and A Study In Crimson**) the definitive **A Chronology of Sir Arthur Conan Doyle**, a biography of **Bertram Fletcher Robinson**, reprint of the novel **Wheels of Anarchy** and the 4 'Lost Playlets of P.G.Wodehouse (**Bobbles and Plum**).

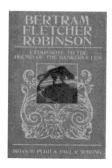  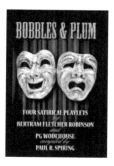

www.mxpublishing.com

Also From MX Publishing

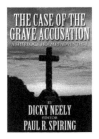

The Case of The Grave Accusation

The creator of Sherlock Holmes has been accused of murder. Only Holmes and Watson can stop the destruction of the Holmes legacy.

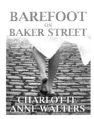

Barefoot on Baker Street

Epic novel of the life of a Victorian workhouse orphan featuring Sherlock Holmes and Moriarty.

Case of Witchcraft

A tale of witchcraft in the Northern Isles, in which long-concealed secrets are revealed -- including some that concern the Great Detective himself!

www.mxpublishing.com

Also From MX Publishing

The Affair In Transylvania

Holmes and Watson tackle Dracula
in deepest Transylvania in this
stunning adaptation by film director
Gerry O'Hara

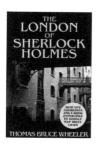

The London of Sherlock Holmes

400 locations including GPS co-
ordinates that enable Google Street
view of the locations around
London in all the Homes stories

I Will Find The Answer

Sequel to Rendezvous At The
Populaire, Holmes and Watson tackle
Dr.Jekyll.

www.mxpublishing.com

Also From MX Publishing

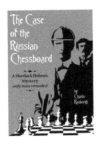

The Case of The Russian Chessboard

Short novel covering the dark world of Russian espionage sees Holmes and Watson on the world stage facing dark and complex enemies.

An Entirely New Country

Covers Arthur Conan Doyle's years at Undershaw where he wrote Hound of The Baskervilles. Foreword by Mark Gatiss (BBC's Sherlock).

Shadowblood

Sequel to Shadowfall, Holmes and Watson tackle blood magic, the vilest form of sorcery.

www.mxpublishing.com

Also From MX Publishing

Sherlock Holmes and The Irish Rebels

It is early 1916 and the world is at war. Sherlock Holmes is well into his spy persona as Altamont.

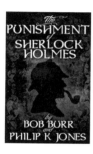

The Punishment of Sherlock Holmes

"deliberately and successfully funny"

The Sherlock Holmes Society of London

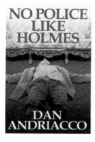

No Police Like Holmes

It's a Sherlock Holmes symposium, and murder is involved. The first case for Sebastian McCabe.

www.mxpublishing.com

Also From MX Publishing

In The Night, In The Dark

Winner of the Dracula Society Award – a collection of supernatural ghost stories from the editor of the Sherlock Holmes Society of London journal.

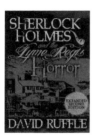

Sherlock Holmes and
The Lyme Regis Horror

Fully updated 2nd edition of this bestselling Holmes story set in Dorset.

My Dear Watson

Winner of the Suntory Mystery Award for fiction and translated from the original Japanese. Holmes greatest secret is revealed – Sherlock Holmes is a woman.

www.mxpublishing.com

Also From MX Publishing

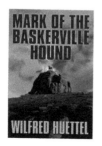

Mark of The Baskerville Hound

100 years on and a New York policeman faces a similar terror to the great detective.

A Professor Reflects On Sherlock Holmes

A wonderful collection of essays and scripts and writings on Sherlock Holmes.

Sherlock Holmes On The Air

A collection of Sherlock Holmes radio scripts with detailed notes on Canonical references.

www.mxpublishing.com

Also From MX Publishing

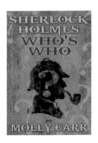

Sherlock Holmes Whos Who

All the characters from the entire canon catalogued and profiled.

Sherlock Holmes and The Lyme Regis Legacy

Sequel to the Lyme Regis Horror and Holmes and Watson are once again embroiled in murder in Dorset.

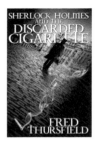

Sherlock Holmes and The Discarded Cigarette

London 1895. A well known author, a theoretical invention made real and the perfect crime.

www.mxpublishing.com

Also From MX Publishing

Sherlock Holmes and The Whitechapel Vampire

Jack The Ripper is a vampire, and Holmes refusal to believe it could lead to his downfall.

Tales From The Strangers Room

A collection of writings from more than 20 Sherlockians with author profits going to The Beacon Society.

The Secret Journal of Dr Watson

Holmes and Watson head to the newly formed Soviet Union to rescue the Romanovs.

www.mxpublishing.com

Lightning Source UK Ltd.
Milton Keynes UK
UKHW020610280619
345207UK00005B/131/P